Porches & Terraces

BY A.J. HARMON, A.I.A.

D1613496

GROSSET
GOOD LIFE
BOOKS

PUBLISHERS • GROSSET & DUNLAP • NEW YORK

Text and illustrations by A. J. Harmon
Cover photograph by Mort Engel

Copyright © 1975 by A. J. Harmon
All rights reserved
Published simultaneously in Canada
Library of Congress catalog card number: 74-33765
ISBN 0-448-12003-8 (trade edition)
ISBN 0-448-13312-1 (library edition)
First printing
Printed in the United States of America

Some of the illustrative material in this book previously appeared in *The Guide to Home Remodeling* by A. J. Harmon, and is reproduced here by permission of Holt, Rinehart and Winston, Inc.

Contents

Porches & Terraces

1
From Roman Atrium
to Southern Veranda

For thousands of years people have enjoyed outdoor living space built onto or into their homes. It is interesting to note that the higher the standard of cultural civilization and the more educated and enlightened the people, the more the freedom and relaxation of outdoor living have been respected and enjoyed. Sadly, the old-fashioned front porch, a singularly American phenomenon, has almost disappeared, along with the horse and buggy. Gone, too, for the most part, are the screened French doors opening onto lush green lawns bordered by quiet residential streets, where one could nod to friends and neighbors strolling by under the shade of lovely old elms. However, even though we have become more security conscious and tend to live in air-conditioned comfort behind closed doors and windows, we still have a great urge to expand our homes to the fresh air and sunlight of the garden.

As we travel and observe the uses that ancient and modern civilizations have made of outdoor living spaces, we bring home ideas and incorporate them into our own particular styles of living. Thousands of years before Christ, Greek and Egyptian homes were built with courtyards and loggias. When the Romans conquered Greece, they did not build any *better* than the Greeks, but they did build *bigger* — spacious central courtyards surrounded on all four sides by rooms leading into them. This type of Roman courtyard was called an atrium. About the same time, or perhaps a little later, the Spanish had the same idea, but they called their courtyards patios. Thousands of years later, Americans began to call any paved area next to a house a patio, a misuse of the word.

Just as the idea of incorporating exterior spaces into homes has come down to us through the ages, so have the terms used to describe the changes in design brought about by each country as it experimented with individual elements to produce a structure that would give people maximum enjoyment according to their manner of living and climate. Thus the Greek court became a Roman atrium, which became a Spanish patio, which developed into a courtyard in England, where the king's private garden came to be called the royal court. Eventually, the people close to the king were referred to as "the court" because they were permitted to use the royal garden. "The court" then was generalized to include not only the king and his nobles, but also, because their

Stoop

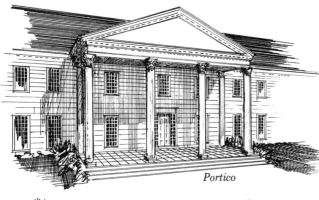

Portico

Colonnade

Gallery

word was the law of the land, the law itself. Our courts and courthouses are etymologically descended from a word used to denote an enclosed living area that is open to the sky.

Porches

Porches are divided into two basic groups, both of which are open to the air, floored, and roofed. One is an expansive area with space for furniture, living, dining, and entertaining. The other is a narrow area used for passage from one place to another and having a specific function.

A porch used for living may be called simply a porch, or a veranda, piazza, solarium, sun room, sun parlor, sun porch, sleeping porch, or Florida room. Basically, these are all the same; the name depends on how the porch is to be used. Veranda, the Hindu word for porch, is used mostly in the South. Piazza is an Italian word meaning the same thing. A solarium is a glassed-in area, usually having glass as all or part of its ceiling. It is more closely associated with hospitals than with houses. A sun room and sun porch are the same thing, glassed and screened rooms used primarily in the spring and fall — but also in the winter, when the sun heats them to a comfortable temperature, and in the summer, when they are cool enough. A sleeping porch — unheated, enclosed or open, and usually on the second floor — may be used the year round, depending on the hardiness of the occupants. A Florida room is a curious American phenomenon — half living room and porch — and half greenhouse.

Porches that are used as passages range from the small stoop, a floored and roofed area in front of an entrance door, to the portico, the roofed and impressively columned entrance to large monumental homes such as Thomas Jefferson's Monticello and the White House. In between are the roofed corridors: the colonnade, open on both sides; the gallery, open on one or both sides and used to display sculpture; the cloister, open on one side and closed on the other, surrounding three or more sides of a courtyard; the porte cochere, a much better designed forerunner of the carport; the loggia, closed in on one side by the house (in the past, it referred to a porch on an upper story of the house that looked down into a courtyard); and, of course, the American breezeway, connecting the garage to the back door.

Terraces

Terraces, on the other hand, are always uncovered and open to the sky, although there may be some temporary construction to shade the pavement from the heat of the sun. A walled courtyard is a terrace with one or two walls formed by the house, and the remaining sides by real walls. If the terrace is surrounded on three sides by the house and on the fourth by a wall, it is a courtyard. When the terrace is within the body of the house and surrounded by it on all four sides, it is a court, an atrium, or a patio.

Outside these classifications are the roof garden, balcony, and deck. All are raised above ground level and protected by a low wall or railing.

For the sake of clarity, throughout this book I will refer to all roofed living areas off the house as porches, all paved open areas as terraces, and all roofed, one-walled passages as loggias.

There are two other classifications of outdoor living areas that I will simply call here garden houses and arbors. An arbor is an open-roofed support for fruit, flowers, or vines. A garden house can be a variety of things. Bowers and casinos are small structures built simply for the fun of having them. A belvedere is a roofed terrace built on a high piece of land or rock overlooking a view. A pergola, which is similar to an arbor, is much more dignified than a bathhouse, but not as sumptuous as a pavilion. A gazebo is a small elegant building, usually octagonal in shape and partially closed. There is also the summerhouse, which can be completely closed or simply walled with a trellis, and the cabana, which can be either simple or elaborate and is used for showering and changing beside a swimming pool.

Porches and terraces do extend the use of our homes. Correctly planned and designed, they will be the main living areas of the house for three to six months of the year. Terraces, how-

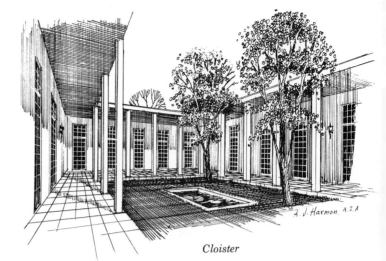

Cloister

Breezeway

Loggia

Porte cochere

From Roman Atrium to Southern Veranda   9

ever delightful they may be on balmy summer evenings, are limited to use in good weather, but they are less expensive to build than porches. If your budget is limited, design the terrace so that all or part of it can be roofed and screened later. Then build additional terraces at different levels for use after the original has been enclosed as a porch. Even though you have a porch, you will want a terrace area off it for cooking out and for children and adults to relax on in fine weather.

If the terrace will probably be roofed and expanded in the future, its placement and design should be considered from that viewpoint in the beginning. A terrace may be placed off the kitchen or living room, but a porch in these locations will become a passageway from the garden to indoors and should be as carefully studied as the rooms themselves for furniture placement, circulation, and exposure.

An entrance porch or terrace has quite a different function than a porch or terrace off a living room or bedroom. It makes a great difference whether it is placed on the north or south side of the house. Privacy from the street and neighboring houses must be considered, along with the view from the terrace, if you are to enjoy using it.

When adding a terrace or a porch, the landscaping is of primary importance, particularly if the addition is at the front of the house. If the property is already well protected from the street, very little will have to be done, except for noise control. But if you have a small lot and the terrace is to be close to the street, it will have to be screened by walls or plantings. You could move the foundation planting to the lot line for privacy and build planters against the side of the house to cover the foundation. You may want to move the front door to a better location if you want the terrace on the side that faces the street.

A terrace off the kitchen can connect the garage to the house and be a pleasant place to have breakfast. It is also a convenient area for children to play under supervision while meals are being prepared.

Terraces and porches off bedrooms are excellent retreats from the more hectic activities in other parts of the house, and they can be much smaller than a terrace off the family or living room.

Building a porch or a terrace anywhere without an overall plan and design for the house and garden is a mistake. You must know how the area is going to be used, by whom, and for how long before you can think seriously of building.

Gazebo

Arbor

Belvedere

2
Legal Regulations

Not all areas of the United States have laws in the form of zoning ordinances and building codes to regulate construction, but most nonrural areas do, and you must comply with the regulations. Cities, townships, and villages have drawn up requirements governing the construction of any new structures, and the alteration of existing buildings, to protect you, your family, and your property. Before you begin planning the addition of a porch or a terrace, investigate the deed restrictions, zoning ordinances, and building codes that regulate construction in your area.

Deed Restrictions

A deed restriction is a condition written into the deed to your property to protect you and your neighbors from unwanted alterations and to maintain a level of continuity in the neighborhood. Deed restrictions may supersede zoning ordinances, so you should reread your deed carefully before you alter the exterior of your house with the addition of a porch or terrace. You may be limited in the use of materials, the type of construction, the area in which you can build, the height, and even the kind of roof you may have.

You may be prohibited from using a flat or a shed roof on an addition, or limited in the choice of roofing material or color. Building restrictions in the deed may state that any new construction or additions to your house must be built of brick. If you are adding a sun porch, the area of glass that may be used in a single unbroken surface may be restricted to prevent your house from taking on a modern character in a traditional neighborhood.

A clause in the deed may prohibit you from building a porch with exposed concrete block, structural steel, or corrugated metal. You may not be allowed to add a porch or terrace to the front or sides of your home. The construction may be limited to a certain percentage of the site so that a portion of the property remains free and open space. This could mean confining yourself to a terrace of a certain size. A deed restriction may also state that you cannot erect a prefabricated tool shed, garden house, or even a gazebo on your property.

Deed restrictions are designed to maintain the character of the neighborhood. They may be dogmatic, but with proper interpretation, they can bring about better neighborhoods with stabilized property values.

Examples of what deed restrictions and zoning ordinances can prevent from happening in your neighborhood.

Zoning Ordinances

Zoning ordinances restrict and define the use of land and buildings for residential, industrial, and business use. Unlike deed restrictions, these ordinances are almost always written for your protection as a property owner. They guard you against having the property across the street from you turned into a motel, a next door neighbor building right up to your property line, or anything that would detract from the value of your house as a residence.

Zoning prevents the construction of chicken coops, stables, commercial food stands, billboards, or anything that might become a neighborhood nuisance. The percentage of the site that can be built on will be regulated, with minimum front, side, and back yards, and some, but not all, porches or terraces may fall within these restrictions.

To determine if you are permitted to add a porch or terrace, you must examine the plot plan or survey of your property. A lot line will establish the outer boundaries of the site, and within this lot line there will be a building line determined by the set-back regulations in the zoning ordinance.

Full-fledged enclosed living spaces must be constructed within the building line, but certain small stoops and porches may encroach on the building line, as determined in the ordinance, without a variance being required. Terraces may usually be built outside the building line, provided they do not have a permanent roof with columns or supports.

The front or side of your house may be the perfect spot for the porch you want, but the zoning ordinance may permit only a terrace in that location. If that is where the outdoor living area can be put to best use, it might be better to settle for a terrace there and add a smaller, but useful, porch in back of the house.

The height of walls at lot lines is controlled, and if you are not permitted to construct a wall high enough to maintain privacy, you might be able to obtain the same effect by erecting a fence on the lot line to obstruct through passage and, on your side of the fence, planting a thick hedge of evergreens whose height is not controlled by the zoning ordinance.

If permitted by the ordinance, temporary

cover for outdoor activities on the terrace might be provided by an awning. Some ordinances permit arbors to be built on the property line, and in that case, if you want something more permanent than an awning, you could construct a light arbor with an open roof over the terrace and plant it with grapes or other vines for shade. If you think insects will be a problem, apply turkey wire to the roof of the arbor to support the weight of the vines and screen in the roof and the sides. Although the arbor will not have all the advantages of a porch, it will comply with the zoning restrictions and you will have a terrace where you and your family will get the best use from it.

A copy of the zoning ordinance is usually available at your town hall or building inspector's office, so get one and familiarize yourself with it before you begin planning. These ordinances can be enforced by fines and the illegal porch or terrace removed if a variance was not obtained beforehand.

Variance

If you feel that you are being too tightly restricted by a particuliar zoning ordinance, you may apply to the zoning board for a variance. If, for instance, the zoning calls for a side yard at least 15 feet from the lot line, but the porch you want to add there will leave a side yard of only 13 feet, you may apply for a variance. The zoning board of appeals meets periodically to review just such cases. After you announce your intentions to your neighbors, your application will come before the board and a public meeting will be called. Anyone objecting to what you are planning to do will be given a chance to voice that objection at the meeting. However, a solution is usually worked out to everyone's satisfaction.

Building Codes

The building code is designed to guarantee minimum safety standards, and will stipulate the minimum size of columns and beams that are needed to support a roof, the size and depth of footings, and so forth. It can also control the design of roofs so they do not collapse under a snow load, blow off in a high wind, or pose hazards in other unusual conditions. The electrical work is also governed by the code, to protect you from electrical fires and shock. If you are required to obtain a building permit, the construction will be checked by a building inspector as the work progresses to ensure it conforms to the code.

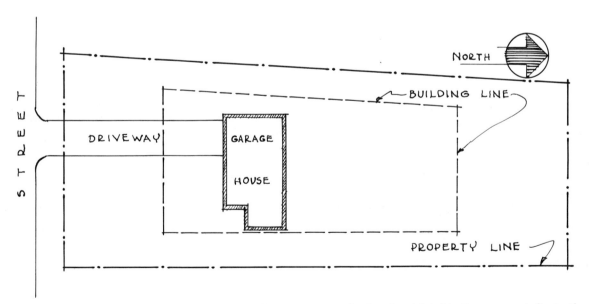

Typical survey or plot plan of your property, to be signed and dated by the surveyor, indicates the allowable buildable area and setback regulations.

Building Inspector

If you do not need a building permit and plan to do the work yourself, the building code will help you erect a safer structure. It is not something to be avoided. The building inspector can advise you on the best and safest way to do things, so ask his opinion and follow his advice concerning any work you plan to do.

If you are having a contractor do the work for you, he may be required to get a building permit and the building inspector will see that everything is properly constructed.

Building Permit

Often it is difficult to know whether you need a building permit. If you hire a contractor to do the work, he will advise you and will apply for a permit if it is necessary. If you plan to do the construction yourself, you may need a permit for any structural work, such as adding a porch where none existed before. But if you are only enclosing an existing porch, a permit is probably not necessary.

Building a terrace does not usually require a permit unless some structural changes are being made to the house to accommodate it. A terrace with an arbor at one end would probably not require a building permit, but a terrace with a gazebo or garden house incorporated into the design would almost certainly require a building permit, as would any other porch or roofed structure.

Whether you do require a building permit or not will depend on the regulations in effect in your area, so consult the building department in your town hall. If you do need a permit, the fee will be based on the estimated cost of construction. Too, the issuance of a building permit almost always assures you of an increased property tax the following year, reflecting the improvement in your house and grounds.

3
The Work—
Who Will Do It, How
to Get It Done

Many houses are greatly enhanced by the addition of a porch or a terrace. On the other hand, some houses are practically ruined, especially when a poorly planned porch is added. A new porch is a structural addition to a home in the same sense as a new room or an entire wing is, and it can change the facade, circulation, and use of the rooms next to it. A porch can make the rooms adjacent to it function better and seem larger, while increasing privacy from the street and within the house itself. If not located properly, though, a porch can turn a living room into a large hallway, and an inconvenient one at that. If a porch that is to be used for dining does not have direct access to the kitchen, so that the food and the dirty dishes have to be hauled to and from the kitchen through the living room, you have not gained a useful porch — in fact, you have lost a good living room.

The location of a new terrace is equally important, though it does not have the same ramifications. The cost of a terrace is less than half that of a porch, and perhaps the worst result of an awkwardly placed terrace is that it simply will not be used.

Next in importance to design is construction. If the floor does not drain away the rainwater, or if the roof leaks constantly, soaking the furniture, a terrace or a porch can become a severe nuisance.

You may feel able to do all the work yourself — both the designing and the actual construction — but most people find at some time during the building process (or sadly, at the end of it when it is too late) that they need some professional help.

The Architect

You may not think you require the services of an architect to design and supervise the construction of a porch or a simple terrace. And you may be right, but the best way to find out is to let the architect tell you. The amount of money you have to spend is no indication one way or the other. In fact, the lower your budget, the more important it is to spend it wisely, getting all you can for the amount you have to spend. An architect will not necessarily save you money, but he will see that you get the most out of your budget, and that the addition is right for you and your house.

An architect will plan, design, find the contractors, and supervise the work for you. Or, if you intend to do the work yourself, he will provide the design and expert advice on the best way to do things with the least expensive materials. He can also help you find the best subcontractors if you want to do only part of the work yourself.

Working with an Architect

Finding an architect is not difficult, but finding one who is willing to take on a small job such as a terrace or porch addition may take time. Call or write the local chapter of The American Institute of Architects and ask for the names of members in your area who do residential work. Or, look up registered architects in the Yellow Pages of your telephone book. Call those who are nearby and tell them your problem. Even if an architect cannot take on the job, chances are he can recommend someone who will be interested.

Make a rough floor plan of your house and take it, and photographs of the exterior, when you go to talk to the architect. He may be able to show you in a rough sketch the best solution — perhaps one you have never thought of — to your problem. It would be even better if you drew your own design and asked him to criticize it and make suggestions. This is a good way to indicate to him what you have in mind and the scope of the work.

An architect will not charge you for a brief discussion, but if he spends much time giving you ideas or sketches, do not expect him to work for nothing. Ask first, and also ask who the best contractors and subcontractors are for the work you need done. He will know because he will have worked with many of them.

If you are going to do all the work yourself, perhaps all you need from the architect is a quick sketch to get you started in the right direction. If more work is required, he will frankly discuss his fee and what you will get for it.

An architect's fee is usually a percentage of the cost of the work, but you may also pay him a set fee established in advance or by the hour. On small jobs, your contract with the architect may consist of a simple letter of agreement, but on more extensive work a standard A.I.A. contract covering all contingencies is better.

When a general contractor is to do the work, an architect will measure the areas involved, draw sketches of what you would like done until you are satisfied with the solution, and then do preliminary drawings to get estimates from several contractors on how much the work will cost. Preliminary bids usually come back too high, so you and your architect will have to sit down together and decide what to eliminate, where to cut corners, and what to simplify. A second preliminary bid is then requested from the contractor you have decided to use. If this falls close to the budget you have worked out, a final set of working drawings is made and given to the contractor for a final price. The architect will settle the contract between you and the contractor, which is usually the standard form of agreement issued by the A.I.A.

The Contractor

You may not need a general contractor. If you have an architect, ask him if between you, you cannot schedule the work and supervise the subcontractors.

Since contractors are not licensed, anyone can hang out a sign and claim to be one — and few have any understanding of planning or design. A contractor simply coordinates the work of carpenters and subcontractors, getting materials and labor to the job at approximately the right time. If he is competent and reliable, however, a good contractor can get the work completed on schedule and with a minimum of frustration.

If you do not have an architect and cannot do the work yourself, finding a good contractor may take months. Many will not consider a job as small as adding a porch or building a terrace. Some firms specialize in porches, dormers, and storm windows, but they are not experienced in design and tend to give you what they can do rather than what you want done or what would be best for your house. Many of them use prefabricated additions, so you will be forced to take what you can get — whether it looks good on your house or not.

You can call local architects and ask them for recommendations, but they will probably be reluctant to give you the names of their best men since good contractors are hard to find and are booked up long in advance. It is better to compile a list of several possible contractors and ask architects which one they think would do the best job.

It is usually a waste of time to check on a contractor or a subcontractor with the Better Business Bureau. They can tell you if complaints have been lodged against any of their members, but joining the Bureau is hardly compulsory. If you or your friends do not know a reputable contractor, a good source may be your lawyer or someone who works at the local courthouse. He may at least know who has been sued lately and how often.

You can try calling lumberyards and building supply companies for possible names, but since they depend mainly on contractors for business, you are not going to hear anything bad about a contractor from them.

Banks and the building department can be good sources of reference, but they, too, usually refrain from unfavorable comments for fear of offending someone or of becoming involved.

After you have obtained the names of as many contracting firms as you can, go around to their offices. If you find a general contractor who works out of his house without an office or secretary, be especially careful. You could go back tomorrow and find he has moved out of town.

A general contractor should have an office, a secretary (not an answering service) to take messages, storage space, and a shop for woodworking. He should own his own home and have been in business in the same town for five to ten years — the longer the better.

Do not worry if his office is a bit shabby and threadbare. A good contractor is too busy working to do much about fixing up his own office. If a contractor has an office impressively decorated with wall-to-wall carpet, walnut paneling, and canned music, forget him. He is trying to impress you with his office — his work may not measure up.

Get the contractor's bank references, the names of the mortgage banks and finance companies that handle his installment loans, and check on them. Find out where he is doing work at the present time and talk to the owners to see if they are satisfied with his work and the men who work for him.

Make sure he carries workmen's compensation, public liability, and property damage insurance. Call his insurance agent and ask how claims are handled. The more you know about a prospective contractor, the better your chances of getting one you will be able to depend on.

Once you have found several contractors you believe can do the work, give them all identical sketches and specifications and let each one know you are getting estimates from other contractors. If after you get back several bids, the contractor you like the most is the highest, ask him if he cannot meet the other bids. You may be able to work out an agreement.

Have a contract drawn up by your lawyer that includes the specifications and the dated sketch you gave the contractor for his bid. Also include in the contract the date work will begin and when it will be finished. Agree to nothing verbally.

Working with a Contractor

On signing the contract, ask the contractor for a work schedule and include it in the terms of the written agreement. The schedule will show when the workmen are to arrive, what they will be doing, and when the plumbing or electricity will be turned off so you can make other arrangements.

Do not follow the contractor or his men around asking questions or making changes in the plans. Keep children and pets away from the workmen and never ask them to answer the telephone or keep an eye on the youngsters while you run into town.

Pay the contractor according to the contract, for labor and materials that *have been installed*. Make the final payment only when the work has been completed as agreed, and to your satisfaction. Once he has been paid off, the contractor may feel the job is finished and will not want to return to patch and fix defective work.

Subcontractors

If you cannot find a general contractor you can trust, you can still have your porch or terrace built by hiring the subcontractors yourself. Although you can save money this way, you may not be able to get the work done as quickly because the subcontractors will have to schedule your work in between the larger jobs they have with general contractors and builders. Since they depend on them for work consistently, but may only work once for you, this is to be expected.

If you are going to act as your own contractor, the best place to start is with a good carpenter — unless you are going to do the carpentry yourself. Good carpenters are even harder to find than good contractors, and they are expensive, but worth it. Carpenters will have worked with the other trades you will need; therefore they will know the best men for the jobs you want done, and can help you coordinate the schedules. Do not hire a carpenter as an employee or you will be responsible for withholding taxes and paying unemployment and workmen's compensation insurance. Draw up a written agreement with him, as with all other subcontractors.

If you decide to do the carpentry yourself, you will have to locate the other trades you need, using the process of bids and elimination.

Talk to your insurance agent to be sure you are fully covered in case of accident. If your garage is not available for the storage of materials, build a fenced storage area so lumber and material can be locked up at night. Things have a way of disappearing, even in the best of neighborhoods, and unless there are signs of forced entry, theft of building materials is not covered by insurance.

When the porch is completed, be sure to increase your insurance to cover the improvement on the house. Since it is worth more, it would cost more to replace in case of fire or some other injury.

4
Money—Where to Invest, How to Borrow

Cost

The least expensive terrace you can build is one on level, well-drained sandy soil, with several wooden steps leading down to it from the door to the house. It would be square or rectangular concrete, and probably very dull. However, do not attempt to make a small flat concrete terrace more interesting by designing it in the commonplace kidney shape. These are, to my mind, even more unattractive. They are certainly more expensive to build, because the form work must be curved, and the kidney shape provides less seating space per square foot than a square or rectangular terrace would.

The most expensive terrace you can build is one of flagstone on two or more levels that slope sharply away from the house. This style requires intricate stairs, retaining walls, and parapets. Cheaper materials may be used, of course, but the real expense is in the retaining walls that are necessary to create flat areas for furniture placement. In between these two extremes is the terrace that will suit you, your house, and your pocketbook.

The simple rectangular concrete terrace can be made much more interesting, for instance, by leaving several holes in it — for a planter, a shade tree, etc. — and you could enlarge it, using the same amount of concrete, at no additional expense. If you cannot afford masonry retaining walls and steps and the ground falls sharply away from the house where you would like a terrace, you can build a wood deck straight out from the house and support it with steel columns. A simple railing made of 2-by-4's will provide adequate protection for the sides.

A terrace can be made less expensive if you never plan to roof it and make it into a porch, but usually this is a saving that should not be made because after the terrace is in, most people find that they would like all or part of it enclosed so they can enjoy it in less than perfect weather.

A porch will cost at least twice as much as a terrace, but you can get more than twice the use out of it. A porch, or a terrace that is going to be made into a porch later, must be more carefully designed than a terrace that will stay a terrace. The mass, the scale, and the roof line will change the appearance of your house. The doors from the house to the porch and the location of the doors from the porch to the garden will change the circulation, not only within the house, but from the house to the garden as well.

With only a few more dollars and a bit of imagination invested, the small paved area (top) can be transformed into an attractive and usable terrace (bottom).

Every porch and terrace should be thought of as part of the garden, and the location should be carefully studied to gain the maximum enjoyment and pleasure from both. There should be a gentle transition from house to porch to terrace to garden and back again.

When you are calculating the expenses involved in the addition of a porch or terrace, it is not enough to consider the cost of construction alone. You must also include in the budget money to provide access from the house to the terrace, which may mean changing a window into a door. And you should anticipate the expenses of furniture, foundation planting, and trees, hedges, or walls to screen out unwanted views either to or from the terrace. Even if you do not do all these things in the beginning, they should be anticipated as future expenditures.

If you can possibly spend the money for some professional help at the very beginning, do so, even if it means financing the cost of the porch or terrace. A bank will be much more inclined to lend you money if you can show them a professionally drawn plan done by an architect or landscape architect.

There are a number of ways to pay for a porch or terrace. The best is probably cash, but there may be instances where this would not be true. It depends on current interest rates and where and how your money is invested.

Financing

The amount you can borrow will depend on your house, the changes that the porch or terrace will make in it, your income, and your credit. To get a loan from any reputable source of financing, you will need a complete set of plans and specifications.

When looking for a loan, start with your own bank and then compare its interest rates and terms with those of other banks. Regulations, rates, and terms change regularly, as do different banks' lending policies. Home improvement loans are sought by most banks because of their high yield of interest.

Home Improvement Loan: Home improvement loans are nonsecured loans, meaning there are no liens placed against the property or the improvement unless the loan goes into default. The bank may send a man to inspect your house, and then the addition when it is completed, to see if the money was spent in accordance with your agreement. At this writing, the interest rates vary from 8 to 12 percent on a government-controlled loan of $10,000 with up to ten years to pay. However, it is not likely you will need anywhere near that size loan, unless you are also doing extensive remodeling on the house.

Mortgage Loan: If you do not have a mortgage on your home, you could apply to a bank for a straight mortgage loan. The interest rate is presently between 8 and 10 percent. The amount of the mortgage will depend on the property, what you plan to do to it, and your financial situation. It is usually a mistake, to take out a mortgage on your home to add a porch or a terrace — unless you are also doing a lot of other work on the house, such as put-

Where rough terrain makes a terrace too expensive to construct, a wooden deck cantilevered over the trees can be an attractive substitute. Architects, Lewis and Harmon, A.I.A.

ting on a new roof or adding a kitchen, bathroom, or heating system.

Mortgage Refinancing: This is a very expensive way of financing and can be used only if you already have a mortgage on your house. The old mortgage must be paid off and a new one drawn up, which will involve lawyers' fees, bank charges, and probably a much higher interest rate than you have been paying. However, if you are doing extensive remodeling on your home, you may want to consider refinancing as an alternative.

FHA (Title I) Loan: Next to paying cash, an FHA Title I Home Improvement Loan may be the best way to pay for the addition of a porch or terrace. This is a loan that is taken out through a regular bank by people who can qualify. If your income is low and your financial situation is such that a bank does not want to lend you money, the Federal Housing Agency may guarantee payment to the bank.

The bank will then lend you the money without risk. (But not all banks will handle FHA loans, so you must find one that will.) The maximum amount you can borrow currently is $2,500 with an interest rate of 9½ percent.

FHA (K) Loan: This is a different kind of FHA loan, and is usually not very suitable for small additions like a porch. K loans are available to those who can qualify at 6 percent interest for a minimum of $2,500 and a maximum of $10,000 with twenty years to pay. The additional charges and fee payments for insurance, service charges, FHA appraisal, and FHA inspections as the work progresses raise the total cost of the loan.

Open-End Mortgage Loan: This kind of loan is a good way to finance a porch or terrace provided you have a mortgage that permits it. An open-end mortgage provides that you may borrow as much money from the bank as you have already paid on your mortgage. Your mortgage will then be increased by the amount borrowed, and the length of time the payments are to be made will be extended.

Personal Loan: These are loans made by commercial banks at interest rates which currently vary from 12 to 18 percent. The maximum amount you can borrow is $10,000 for a minimum of three years. In spite of the high interest rates, excellent credit and references are required.

Finance Company Loan: These loans are available to almost everyone and are usually used to buy automobiles, furniture, and television sets. You should not take such a loan to add a porch or terrace to your house because the interest rates are very high, usually 14 to 18 percent on a maximum loan of $2,500. High-pressure home-improvement salesmen carry finance company forms with them, and will try to get you to sign them to pay for work the salesman wants you to let his company do on your house. Never sign anything without having your lawyer or your bank look it over first.

Credit Union Loan: If you belong to a credit union, it will be a good source of money to finance an addition if the work is not too extensive. Credit union terms and rates are usually generous, although there is a limit to the amount you can borrow.

Insurance Company Loan: You may be able to borrow on your insurance to pay for the porch or terrace, although this is probably not the best or least expensive way to finance the improvement. In any loan, read the fine print and be aware of hidden costs, add-on charges, and the true amount of interest you will be paying. Even if your bank would not give you a loan, it will usually be glad to explain loans from other sources.

5
Building a Terrace

It is difficult to imagine a home that could not benefit from the addition of a terrace, or a family whose life would not be richer with one. A terrace is the least expensive living area you can add to your home. It can actually cost less than a good lawn, and maintenance varies from minimum to nothing, yet its uses vary from the functional to the strictly ornamental.

The terrace need not be next to or part of the house. It can be isolated from the traffic and circulation of your home to become simply a focal part of the garden, or an ornamental setting for a fountain or sculpture to be admired from the porch or living room. A terrace may be built as a quiet retreat at the far end of the garden, a shaded secret place offering the seclusion of the tree house that each of us longed to build in childhood. Or the terrace you build could replace your living room, dining room, and kitchen during a good part of the year — giving you a place for the children to play and the adults to relax in the sun, a place to cook over charcoal, and dine in the open air at sunset. A terrace can and should be something more than just a flat paved area outside the sliding glass doors of your living room.

Of course, a terrace has some disadvantages. It can be used only half the year in most parts of the country. It offers no protection from the burning sun in summer, no shelter from the rain or cold winds, and can look bleak and dreary on cold snowless winter days. However, unless it had these drawbacks, it would not be warmed by the sun in early spring, cleaned by the rain all year, and cooled by the breeze on hot summer nights. No other addition will do as much for as little money.

With proper planning and design, you can minimize the disadvantages and make the most of the positive aspects of a terrace, whether it is on the north or south, east or west side of the house; whether it is on the front, back, or side; whether the ground slopes up from the house, or down and away from it; whether the ground is flat and lifeless, or heavily wooded and seemingly impossible to clear. The type and design of the terrace will depend on its location and how you would like to use it. A terrace should be planned and designed as carefully as a room, with heating, cooling, lighting, privacy, and circulation all taken into consideration so that it is a definite contribution to your way of living and to the value of your house and property.

Almost every terrace can be improved with protective walls. Here, plants and flowers flourish on the north wall facing the terrace and the sun. Rough wooden gates close and lock for security.

On the South

A southern exposure is preferred for northern hemisphere terraces because it is the south side of the house that receives the most sun from morning until evening. Too, in the winter, a terrace allows the sun to warm southern exposure rooms, whereas a porch roof would block out the sun. In the summer, when the hot sun may not be so welcome, deciduous trees offer the best and most permanent shade for a terrace. Since they lose their leaves in the fall, the use of the terrace can be extended during the day well into Indian summer.

If there are no trees to shade the terrace, you can plant fast-growing ones. Build a temporary shelter from the sun using lath, snow fence, awnings, or plastic, until the trees can take over the job.

Another reason the south side of the house is the preferred location for a terrace is that it is protected from the cold winds that come from other directions. A southern exposure allows you to use the terrace earlier in the spring and later in the fall. This is particularly desirable if you are going to the expense of building a swimming pool and want to incorporate a terrace with it.

On the North

A terrace on the north side of the house has the advantage of being much cooler during the hottest part of the summer, but this very advantage shortens its season. Because the sun's rays are low in early spring and late fall, a good part of the terrace will be in shade in those seasons, and cool breezes, while welcome in July and August, will chase you indoors during May and October.

A terrace on the north, however, especially if protected by a fence, hedge, or wall at the northern end, is perfect for enjoying spectacular displays of perennial or annual flowers because they will get the full sun. Flowers grown at the far end of a southern terrace, on the contrary, will turn their backs on you to face the sun.

To extend the use of a terrace on the north side of your house, separate it from the house wall with a wide entrance path leading to it so that most of the terrace gets the full sun most of the year.

On the East

If you are an early riser and like the sun, a terrace on the east side of the house could be very enjoyable. It is ideal for breakfast in summer before the coolness of the night gives way to the heat of the sun. An eastern terrace will also be cool in the evening because it will have been shaded by the house a good part of the day, especially from the hot late afternoon rays.

Most flowers and plants do best with morning sun, and morning glories planted on the east will be awake and blooming two hours before those on any other side of the house. So, if you like a morning stroll to see the flowers, then a cup of coffee with a quick glance through the paper, build your terrace on the east. This location cannot be improved on for starting or finishing a hot summer day.

Unless protected by walls or hedges, however, your season in the sun will be short. Some of our worst weather and coldest winds come from the east. Psychologically, though, the east side of the house is usually the quietest and most restful. Perhaps this is because the sun passes over it early, and the morning glories are getting ready for sleep at five o'clock in the afternoon.

On the West

Terraces on the west side of the house can seem too warm even in the morning, when they are still in shade. Usually this is because the paving is still giving off the heat it absorbed the day before. Most plants and flowers do not do particularly well on the western side of the house because it is difficult to shade them from the full force of the late afternoon sun, although plants growing along the far end of the terrace, against a fence or wall, will get the full benefit of the morning sun and will do well if sheltered from the wind.

A terrace on the west has two advantages and one disadvantage. The two advantages are

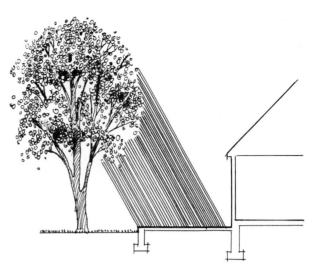

Deciduous trees planted on the south side of a terrace will protect it from the hot sun in summer.

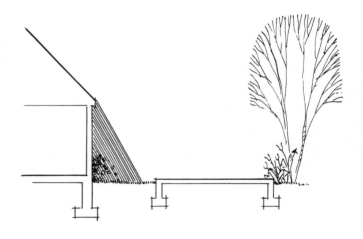

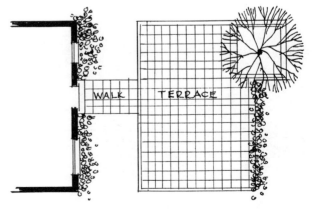

A terrace on the north side of a house, shown here in section and plan, can be warmed by the sun if removed from the wall of the house and connected by a walk.

Because of the slope up from the house this is a difficult site for a terrace.

Space can be provided for a terrace on a slope up from the house by building a retaining wall to contain the hillside.

spring and fall. It will be warmer in the afternoon, earlier in the spring and later in the fall than any other location, and it will be usable in the evenings until late October or early November. The disadvantage is midsummer. It will take very careful planning to make a western terrace usable in the summer from afternoon until sometimes well after dark, when it has finally cooled off. But spring, fall, and even winter sunsets can be enjoyed from a terrace on the west side of the house, which can make it incomparable, as long as it is protected from the stiff northwest breeze.

On Difficult Sites

Usually a terrace does not work out to face the compass points as neatly as those just described, so yours may end up with some of the advantages and disadvantages of different locations. The terrain will also exercise considerable leverage in the design of your terrace. You may think a rocky hill or a heavily wooded slope up to or away from the side of the house makes a terrace impractical where you would like to have it. But regardless of the complications, a terrace is always feasible, and usually, the more difficult the site, the more interesting and attractive the solution.

On a Slope Up from the House

Depending on the angle of the slope (and also on how badly you want to be able to walk directly out of the house right onto the terrace), there are two ways of solving the problem. If direct access is of primary importance, then the slope will have to be regraded and the earth held back with a retaining wall or a series of railroad ties, old telephone poles, or small dry walls made of loose rock or concrete block at an angle of 45 degrees from the horizontal. The floor of the terrace should slope away from the house wall and be drained to a dry well to prevent flooding and a damp basement. These precautions — retaining walls and drains — can be expensive. But you can certainly create a very dramatic setting, especially if the terrace and the slope are on the south side and you want to open the area to allow more sun to enter the house.

A less expensive way to build a terrace in this situation (and in many ways just as interesting) is to construct several lower retaining walls or banks and place the terrace away from the house, on a higher level on the slope. You can build an approach to the terrace from the house with wide steps, always being careful to drain groundwater around and away from the first-floor and basement walls. If the house is two stories high, an interesting addition could be a balcony off a bedroom with a small staircase down to the terrace so it can be reached easily from both floors of the house. The balcony could also protect the doors leading to the terrace from the first floor.

On a Slope Away from the House

In many ways, this situation is the easiest and least expensive for a terrace, because in the first place there is no problem of drainage to consider, and secondly, the terrace can provide so much more than just outdoor living space. Basically, there are four possibilities.

If your house is built on a crawl space, you can simply build a retaining wall at the edge of the terrace location and fill it with earth. After waiting for it to settle sufficiently, then build the terrace floor on the fill. Or, if the slope is heavily wooded and very steep, you can leave the hill and trees untouched by building a self-supporting deck out from the house, leaving holes for the trees to grow through the wood deck. You must remember to clean the brush and loose leaves out from under the deck each year to reduce the danger of fire.

If your house is built on a basement, you can level a terrace area halfway between the high and low levels of the slope, using the earth from one half to fill the other. This will be less expensive because the retaining wall is half the height, but more importantly, you will be able to open the basement walls for additional windows, providing more light and ventilation there. The terrace will have to be approached by a broad stair, which will only make it more interesting.

Less expensive to construct than a retaining wall is a series of smaller walls for a terrace approached from the house by steps. If the house is two stories high, access could be obtained from the second floor by the use of steps and a balcony.   Architects, Lewis and Harmon, A.I.A.

On a slope away from the house a cantilevered deck may be the least expensive solution.

If you would really like to go all the way with a terrace off the living room and a second one off the basement, you can excavate the slope to the level of the basement floor and put in a sliding glass door from the basement to the ground-level terrace. On top of the ground-level terrace, you can build a self-supporting deck reached from the first floor of the house by a bridge — a very exciting approach indeed. You may also want to add a stair from the basement terrace to the deck so it can be used from both levels. This is not inexpensive, but so much is gained: a terrace, deck, covered colonnade, marvelous garden area, plus excellent livable space in an otherwise dark and dreary basement.

On an Intersecting Slope

When the best location for the terrace is at the side of the house, but the slope intersects, there are two obvious solutions. You can build either a self-supporting deck, leaving both the upper and lower sides open, or a stepped terrace on at least two different levels. If you decide on the less expensive deck, you may want to make it accessible from ground level by building a small bridge. Again, the area under the deck should be kept cleared of brush and everything except ground cover to avoid the possible spread of ground fire.

A two-level terrace will involve the use of retaining walls of railroad ties, telephone poles, dry walls of masonry, or regular masonry to shore up the slope. If not held back, the slope will constantly wash down over the terrace, making it difficult to keep clean. Creosoted timber can sometimes be used to retain the bank, if placed at the steepest natural grade of 45 degrees and planted with ground cover to hold the soil. Access from the basement would be difficult to devise in this situation, unless the slope is so steep that the outer edge of the basement floor is already at grade. In that case, a stair to the deck or terrace is not hard to design or construct.

On a slope away from the house many possibilities exist for providing a terrace and for opening the basement to light and air with its own outdoor living area.

6
The Best Terrace in the Right Place

It does not really matter where the terrace is going to be in relation to the terrain — any site can be made to accommodate a terrace. But the location and intended use of the terrace will determine its practicality. Hills, rocks, trees can all be overcome with careful planning; privacy, security, and easy maintenance can be assured. The room or rooms of the house that will open onto the terrace will be the deciding factor in how the terrace is used. You may want to have two smaller terraces instead of one large one — one off the living room and kitchen for entertaining, outdoor cooking, and children's activities, and another small private terrace off your bedroom for quiet relaxation. Each terrace should be designed for what it is to accomplish. A quiet bedroom terrace should ensure privacy above all else, but it should also be secure to prevent forced entry. However, the materials do not need to be nearly as rugged as those used in a more exposed and active area, such as a terrace off the family room. Each should be considered separately.

Entrance Terrace

An entrance terrace is generally not used for relaxing, dining, or entertaining. It is simply a way to get from the driveway or street to the front door without getting your shoes muddy. It should be simple, severe, obvious, and point the way to the door if that cannot be seen from the driveway. It should be well lighted and of the same character as the house. It may be, however, that your living room is on the south side of the house, along with the entrance, and that that is the ideal place for the terrace, even though it faces the street. If your house is level with the street, the answer is a high fence softened by privet and vines, or a wall for privacy, quiet, and security. The zoning ordinance will tell you the allowable height of any wall or fence, but usually there is no limit to the height of a hedge unless it is right on the front property line.

If your house is not constructed on the allowable building line, you can build a wall or fence at the building line to a height of 8 feet or more (at the building line you might be restricted to a height of 4 feet, which offers no privacy or security). A high wall is preferable — especially if the terrace is to be at the front of a house next to a street — even if that means your terrace must be

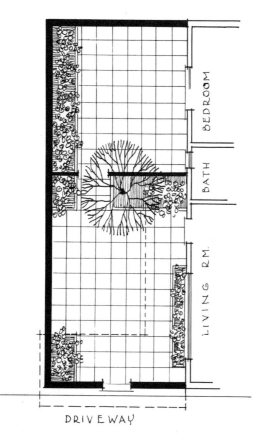

Even a house on a narrow lot next to the street can have a private terrace with the use of walls, as shown here in plan and perspective.

made long and narrow. Various designs can be used that will not restrict the free passage of air to cool the terrace in the summer.

A 9-foot-wide terrace protected by a high wall is much more usable than a 16-foot-wide terrace that lacks privacy. If, as in so many development houses, there is a bedroom at the front of the house, it, too, can be opened onto the terrace, which can be separated from an entrance terrace by another, more open wall. The entrance area can be roofed over on two edges, and the small projection will protect the door to the driveway, in effect creating a new entrance.

More rambling suburban houses, not confined to so narrow a lot, may have a more formal front entrance terrace with French doors opening onto it from the rooms along the south front of the house facing the street. The street should be far enough away so that privacy is not a problem. Planting should be concentrated along the front property line. Security and ventilation can be ensured by louvered shutters that may be closed at night.

Of course, either one of these methods may also be used to advantage when the entrance is at the back of the house, away from the street, although here you may be concerned only with privacy from the sides and back of the lot.

If your house is on a hill above the street, privacy and security may be provided, along with some sound insulation, by a deck with a solid railing. The hard edge of the railing can be softened with planting boxes and vines.

When you want the terrace on a side of the house that is below street level, heavy planting and fencing are just about the only answer. If there is very little space for planting, an arbor would provide privacy from the street for part of the terrace and shade it in the summer, but if the space is too tight, an arbor may cut down on the circulation of air between the house and the side of the hill.

Terrace lighting should not shine onto the street and, except for the front door, should not be bright. All stairs and changes in level, however, should be well lighted.

Living Room Terrace

Living room terraces tend to be the largest because the living room is normally the biggest room in the house. In summer, the terrace will be used instead of the living room. If possible, provide an entrance to the terrace from the hall or driveway so that you do not have to go through the living room every time you wish to use the terrace. Otherwise, you will find tennis rackets, catcher's mitts, wet towels, and footprints from bare feet in the living room.

The living room terrace should also connect to the kitchen door to provide easy serving of cool drinks and snacks. If these are brought through the living room, the sliding or hinged screen door is almost inevitably going to get the better of a nervous host and a balanced tray of iced tea. It is easier to clean the kitchen floor than the living room carpet.

There should be a light beside every door to illuminate thresholds, and a light over all steps. But, in general, lighting should be very subdued and directed toward the garden, not the house wall. If you have electrical outlets for a tape player or other portable appliance, they should be waterproof and of the type approved by the Fire Underwriters Association for ex-

terior use. A hose bib should be close at hand for cleaning the surface of the terrace.

If noise from a highway or street will be annoying, include a small fountain to cover the street sounds. A small electrical pump will recirculate the water from a shallow pool, which can be filled from the hose.

Furniture for the terrace should be simple, heavy enough not to blow around in storms, but light enough to be moved easily. Wrought iron will outlast just about everything, but it is too heavy to be stored easily in the winter and is very expensive. Lighter-weight and more modern iron furniture is also expensive, but it can be moved and stored easily. Wicker is lovely, but will not hold up unless painted every year or two. Wood also will have to be painted to last. The typical unpainted redwood garden furniture deteriorates quickly — not the wood itself, but the metal screws and rods used to hold it together. Combinations of aluminum and plastic vary from the cheap versions you can buy at the grocery store every spring (which is just about how often you will have to buy this kind of furniture) to the very expensive. The thing to look out for in aluminum furniture is sharp corners that can cut unprotected areas of the body.

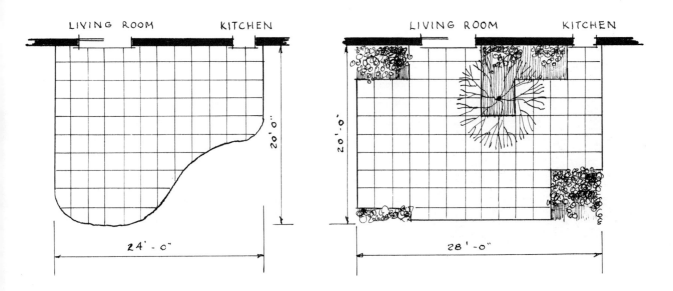

The same amount of area used for a terrace can be used well or badly depending on the design.

Dining Room Terrace

A terrace off the dining room almost always means you are going to be serving breakfast, lunch, and dinner there every chance you get. So, of course, a dining room terrace must be connected to the kitchen, and probably to the living room as well. It should be as large or larger than the dining room itself, because you will want several lounge chairs and conversation groups of furniture. An outdoor table can be used, but since it takes up so much space, it is usually better to have only a serving table and folding trays for informal dinners.

The same things said about living room terrace furniture apply here. If you do want a large outdoor dining table with a glass top, do not get clear plate glass that you can see through. Instead, buy translucent glass so you will not have to sit through dinner staring at knees and feet. Too, translucent glass is easier to keep clean. If there are small children in the family, get wire glass or tempered glass.

An outdoor grill for cooking is an excellent way of getting out of the kitchen on a hot sum-

mer night. If the garage is handy, you can always roll a portable grill into it and continue cooking there when a sudden storm comes up just as you are about to turn the hot dogs. An open garage is a good adjunct to any terrace, perfect for quick cover when it rains, and a lean-to can be built as storage for the terrace furniture when not in use.

A masonry grill can be a handsome addition to a dining terrace, not only for cooking but also to take the chill off a cool night. For additional heat, you could run copper pipes filled with antifreeze through the grill and into the concrete terrace floor. This would extend the use of your terrace a month in each direction, and is an excellent start on an enclosed porch for the future.

A masonry grill ought to have some sturdy protection or a sudden shower may ruin your cookout. A brick or stone grill is permanent, but since the breeze is not, do not build one until you are sure in which direction the smoke will go most of the time. Utmost care must be exercised in locating the grill or smoke will settle around your guests on a hot, muggy, windless summer evening.

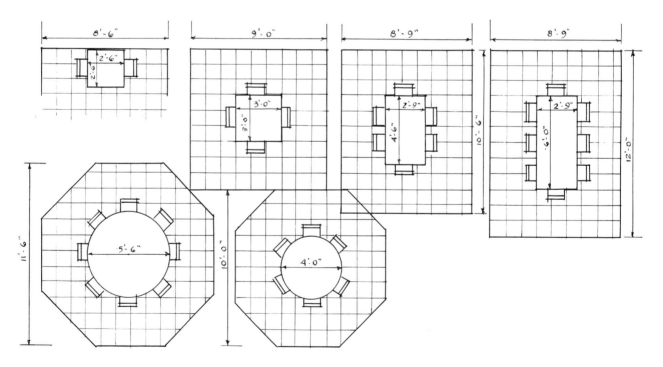

Areas required for dining table and chairs.

Concrete is best for both dining room and living room terraces because it is easy to clean, can be freshened with paint, is smooth to walk on (with no uneven breaks to trip a toddler or the elderly), and easy to push the furniture aside on to clear space for dancing and games. On or near a dining terrace there should be a hose bib for easy cleaning and also for safety's sake since you are going to be using charcoal fires.

Electric lighting must be provided for all thresholds and steps, but should be of low density and on the perimeter of the terrace, where it will attract insects away from the hurricane lamps on the dining or serving table. Insects usually will not fly near a light over the grill because of the heat and smoke. At least one double outdoor outlet should be placed near the serving table so you can plug in electrical appliances such as a coffeepot or hot plate.

Kitchen Terrace

A kitchen terrace should have a more strictly utilitarian function than the ones we have talked about so far. Though it should be nice enough for breakfast or a family lunch, it would not usually be used for entertaining. It should be built off the kitchen and driveway, with convenient access to the garage and garbage cans, which would preferably be placed on the driveway side of the planting. Use inconspicuous garbage cans buried in the ground with a concrete platform around them if you can possibly afford to. You will not have to look at unsightly cans and they will pay for themselves over the years in being protected somewhat from weather, damage, theft, and possible loss on windy days. They would also be inaccessible to neighbors' dogs and other little creatures that like to turn them over.

A kitchen terrace should have space for an herb garden along the north side, where it will get full sun. There should also be a clothesline for drying laundry in the sun on nice days. Have a table and chairs and a small grill so the children can prepare their own hamburgers for lunch and have their own outdoor picnic when adults are using the living room or dining room terrace.

If you like to work in the garden, try to allocate space for a potting table, with room under it for tools, clay pots, watering can, and extra hose and sprinklers. Fertilizers and sprays should not be stored here, but in a locked closet where children cannot get to them. Include a combination hose bib and cold-water faucet for washing hands and home-grown vegetables. You might also want to have an outdoor shower for the children to wash sand or grass off wet feet when they return from swimming or tennis, or even for giving Spot (Rover, Duke, Missy, Queenie) his or her spring and fall baths.

Since it will probably not be used at night, lighting could consist of one or two lights for taking out the garbage on summer and winter nights after dark, and for seeing who might be at the back door. Plants and walls should screen the kitchen terrace from the street and from the more formal living and dining room terraces.

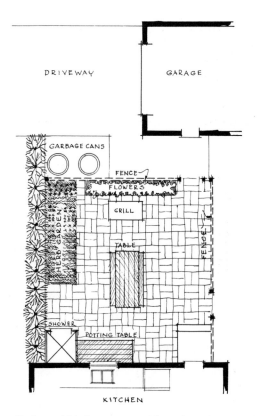

A well-planned kitchen terrace with outdoor shower and potting table.

Bedroom Terrace

A small private terrace off the master bedroom might seem a selfish indulgence at first, but will prove more and more worthwhile. Just spend a night at a motel where each room has a private balcony or secluded terrace to see how much you will enjoy having one. Privacy and security are the most important considerations for a bedroom terrace because you will want to leave the doors to it open during much of the year. There should be a locked door or gate on the garden side so that the terrace can be tended without having to go through the bedroom to get to it.

A bedroom terrace can be quite small — just large enough to hold a lounge, a small table, and two chairs for Sunday morning coffee. Lighting, except for a security light, will probably not be needed, although a small light beside the door to illuminate the threshold is advisable.

Materials can be much less durable than those used for other terraces because a bedroom terrace will not get much traffic or heavy use. But remember, whatever material you use should feel pleasant under your bare feet. (This would preclude the use of gravel, since it is hard to walk on and could be tracked into the bedroom.) You should also include a hose bib so the terrace can be cleaned easily.

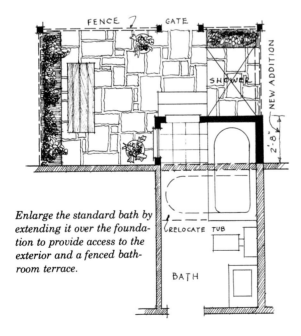

Enlarge the standard bath by extending it over the foundation to provide access to the exterior and a fenced bathroom terrace.

Bathroom Terrace

A terrace off a bathroom must have a door to it from the bathroom itself if it is to be used properly and to its fullest extent. There should also be a door in any walls or hedges separating the bathroom terrace from the garden so that access to the bathroom will be from both within and outside the house. This can be a big advantage if you have lots of small children around.

The minimum 5-by-8-foot bath can be changed in several ways to accommodate a door. First and easiest is to replace the bathtub with a shower and add a door to the exterior, but this still leaves you with a minimum bath. A second way to add a door is to cantilever the floor of the bathroom over the footing by the few feet required to add a tub in a new location (this will not require any plumbing changes). Many building codes will permit you to do this even though the existing footing is on the building line.

A more extensive change could be the addition of a shower and the relocation of the bathtub. You might also want an outdoor shower, which will cost very little to add. Depending on the pitch, a new roof could simply be extended, perhaps using a skylight, over the terrace area. Especially if the terrace is poured concrete, this can be a very inexpensive addition.

The bathroom terrace should be small, but not too small for comfortable sunbathing. It should have a drain and hose bib in it for easy cleaning. Complete privacy can be maintained with a privet hedge or evergreens screening a chain-link fence, or, if the code permits, a ventilated wall of wood or concrete block.

You may want to shade the terrace from the summer sun with a roofed trellis or vines. You could also improvise your own natural sauna by roofing solid walls with ventilating skylights to trap the heat of the sun, although this additional heat might make it necessary to put a ventilating fan in the bathroom to keep it from becoming uncomfortably warm.

Electrical fixtures should be simple and should be controlled from an area away from tub, shower, or terrace, where contact between water on the floor and the outlet could cause shock.

Basement Terrace

A terrace off the basement is neither impractical nor improbable and can do a great deal to improve the use of the basement. If the house is on a hill or slope, the situation is less complicated because all you need do is grade the level of the soil away from the basement walls. Before you start digging, inspect the property, the site plan, and the utility lines to be sure that you will not run into any underground pipes.

The earth outside the basement may be leveled to expose only the top half of the basement to additional sunlight and air. If there are problems with sewage lines or pipes, high-water tables, or drainage, this may be the best way to create a basement terrace. It will, however, be halfway between the basement floor and the first floor of the house, and therefore cannot be fully used from the basement. But it will allow additional light into the basement, which in itself is an advantage.

Even if the area around your house is flat, you can build a terrace off the basement by excavating below the basement floor and, using retaining walls on three sides and reinforcing the basement footing, opening the basement to

the terrace with sliding glass or French doors. A drain should be placed in the terrace floor to keep water from backing into the basement during rain or snow storms.

Walls, fences, and foundation should be placed at the top of the wall to prevent stray animals and strangers from stumbling onto the terrace floor. A stair could be built along one wall to allow the basement terrace to be used in conjunction with another terrace on that side of the house.

You may not want access to the basement terrace from the exterior of the property. In that case, you can provide a second exit with an exterior stair to a private balcony or porch protecting the basement doors.

Because of the need for retaining walls, this is an expensive terrace to build, but considering what it can do for a basement room, it may well be worth the expense. It will also make bedroom doors and windows left open at night during the summer inaccessible from the grounds so that anyone sleeping in those rooms can rest securely. Knowing that strangers cannot enter through flimsy screen doors and windows will cut down on the use of air conditioners during the summer months.

A terrace off the basement can be an important addition to the house and provide additional security for first-floor bedroom windows.

Swimming Pool Terrace

Terraces around a swimming pool are a must to keep dirt and grass out of the pool. While they should be designed as part of the pool, they should also retain some relation to the house since during summer months the pool will be an important focus of activity and circulation.

One end of the terrace, usually the area around the shallow end of the pool where small children are more apt to be playing, should be made large enough for lounges, chairs, and tables for relaxing and parental supervision. Since cool drinks and snacks are a part of outdoor summer living, it is best if this area is close to either the kitchen or a bathhouse (wherever the nearest refrigerator is located).

Terraces around swimming pools should be slip-proof and safe. If concrete is used, it should have a brushed, not a smooth-floated, finish. It may be painted to make it more attractive and fresh looking, but an exterior slip-proof paint should be used because over the years regular paint will fill in the rough surface and allow it to become slippery. If you intend to paint a concrete terrace or any other concrete construction, wait at least six months for the concrete to fully cure or the paint will not adhere to it.

Wood decks, although many times less expensive (especially around raised plastic pools) should not be used. Wood will become slippery and, because of the constant dampness around the pool, will support the growth of fungi, which are themselves very slippery even when the wood is dry. Too, even the best wood will splinter. Painted wood decks, while less likely to splinter or support bacteria, are slippery when wet, even when a slip-proof paint has been used.

All pools should be fenced or walled (this is usually controlled by the zoning ordinance) even if you live in the country ten miles from your nearest neighbor. Your pool will be safer and you will get more use out of it and the terrace if it is protected from cool winds.

7
Building a Porch

In some ways, the problems that arise when planning a porch are similar to those that come up when designing a terrace. These are: exposure, terrain, prevailing breeze, privacy, security, and utility. In addition, the porch has more far-reaching effects on the rooms within the house — the light and air they receive — and the circulation of activity may have to be changed to provide access to a porch through a door that was formerly a window. You may find that in adding a porch off a sunny room you have made that room into a relatively dark hallway, or that a good furniture arrangement no longer works because of the circulation through the room to the porch. A terrace will expand a house physically, and low walls and screening can improve the house structurally to some extent, but the addition of a porch with a roof will influence the size and appearance of a house architecturally and can change its entire exterior character as well as the way it is lived in.

Since a porch is considerably more expensive to build than a terrace, it is only natural to expect more from it in terms of use and convenience. And, just as a terrace should serve more than one function, do more for your way of living than provide a paved open area to place a chair on from time to time, a porch should be the center of your family's activities for more than half the year. It should also make your house look better, enhance your lifestyle, and contribute to the value of your property.

To design a porch properly, study materials, proportions, roof lines, and circulation. The porch should not look tacked on, but rather as if it had been designed and built with the house — as if without it the house would be incomplete. A porch should also work with the existing rooms of the house to extend their usefulness without making them into connecting hallways during the summer and dark, interior, unused rooms in the winter.

The porch will be an important area of living in the summer, but since you use your living room a great deal in winter, the porch should not be allowed to overshadow it, as often happens when a porch is added to the southern side of a living room. Such a porch will keep the living room cooler in summer, but will also tend to make it gloomy in the winter when you want warm sunlight in the house. This is one reason why the south side of the house is not always the best location for a porch. Another is that someday you may want to enclose the

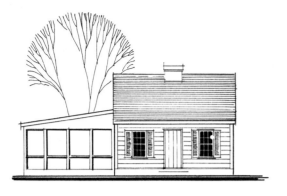 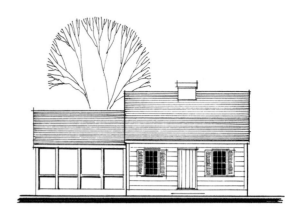

The design of the porch roof will exert considerable effect on the facade of the house.

 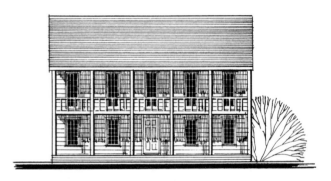

Additional bedroom space can be designed into the roof of the porch for very little additional cost.

A second floor porch provides security and protects the bedroom's doors and windows from sun and rain.

porch and make it into interior living space, so if right from the beginning you plan as if you are going to do just that, you will get a better porch and make a better investment. Insulate the ceilings and any solid walls that will be covered during the original construction so that if you decide to enclose it in the future, this work will already have been done. And if you have a two-story house, make the columns and roof joist large enough to support a second-floor porch or deck whether you want to add one now or in the future. It costs so little more and can add so much to the pleasure you derive from your home.

One thing more about porches before we get down to some facts. Everyone knows that as the years pass, a person becomes tired, fades a bit, shows the beginnings of crow's-feet about the eyes, develops chins and spare tires that were not there twenty years ago. The same thing is true of some houses. The basic structure may be sound, but additions have been made from time to time, usually not in the best interests of design. The years and weather will have had their way with the exterior, and although they could be interesting houses, they have begun to show their age. A woman could wear a veil in strong sunlight to soften the illu-

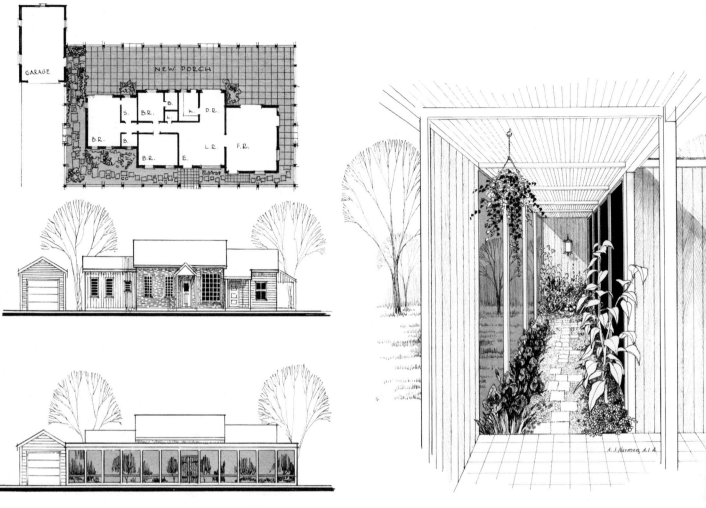

A screened porch on all four sides of the house can unify a facade and at the same time provide excellent outdoor living space.

Inside the screened area, even narrow passages become interesting garden corridors.

sion; a man could have a hairpiece made up. A screened porch added to all four sides of your house can also work to great effect, not only changing the apparent facade, but also the way you live in the house.

Two, or even three, sides may be as narrow as 4 feet. The screened area may be used as landscaped and planted paths allowing you to walk around the house or from one porch to another under cover. And the screened walks and porches will serve another purpose. They will allow you to do away with individual screened doors and windows so that air can circulate around and through the house freely.

The 4-foot roofed area will keep the hot summer sun out of the house, but permit winter sun to enter. It will shield open windows from rain and sudden showers, so you will not have to rush around the house in the middle of the night closing windows or dash home in midday. And if you are at home, you can just relax and enjoy the rain. So you can give your house an inexpensive face lift, gain several screened porches, improve the heating and cooling systems and the way the house is lived in, and at the same time be protected from rain, snow, sun, and insects with an all-encompassing screen.

On the South

A southern exposure is preferred for most terraces, but the south may not be the best location for a porch because the porch may shade the windows of an important room in the winter, leaving it a dark uninviting space enjoyable only after nightfall, when you must turn on the lights anyway. However, a porch will be most useful on the south because there it will get more sun in the spring and fall and be protected by the house from rain and other bad weather from the north. To many people, the south side is an unbeatable location, and placing a porch on any other side of the house is out of the question. If you are one of these people, take all precautions in the design to see that you do not block the sun from the adjoining rooms during the winter.

The seriousness of the problem will depend on which room adjoins the porch, when it is used, for what purpose, and what other exposures it has that could become sources of sunlight. If the porch is to be off a dining room that

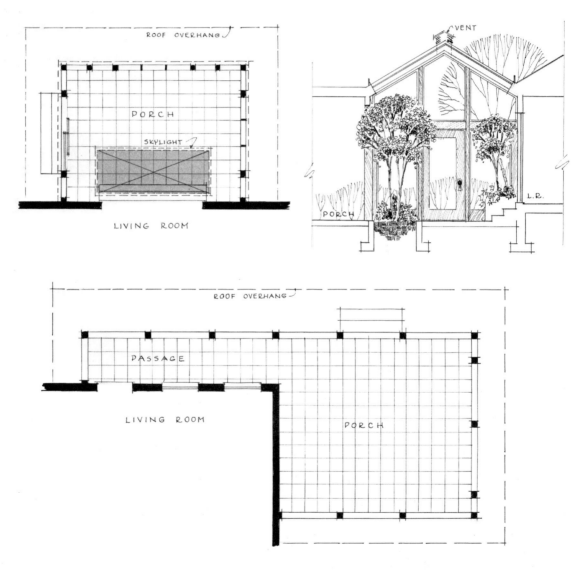

Porches added to the south side of a house do not have to shade the interior if designed with a skylight, separated by a greenhouse structure, or connected to the house by a passage.

is not used very much during the day, it may not matter that the addition will keep sunlight out in winter. But if it is to be off a living room or family room where sunlight is important during the day in winter, you will have to design the porch so that both it and the room will get winter sunlight.

This could be accomplished by providing a skylight in the roof of the porch over the existing doors and windows. You might even want to consider connecting the porch to the house with a greenhouse-like structure whose double glass walls would insulate the living room from the cold in the winter and the porch from noise in the summer. It is often possible to connect the porch to the preferred room by running a narrow screened passage along the exterior wall, which will permit winter sun to enter both the room and the porch if you decide to glass it in at a later date.

Porch walls are not that expensive, since about all they amount to are some posts and screen, so you could place the porch at a distance from the house, creating a small courtyard so that all three could benefit from the winter sun. This can be especially effective if you live in a crowded neighborhood and are tired of looking at your neighbor's yard. A porch stripped of furniture and accessories is not the most attractive view from a window in winter; a courtyard can block this scene. The porch should be connected to the house with a screened passage, which will not add that much to the cost.

If you have a two-story house and want to add a porch on the south, you may want to consider making the porch two stories high. In this case, you could build the porch against the house wall, and the only added expense would be for the extra length of the columns and screening. This would permit the first-floor rooms to get plenty of sunlight in winter, and skylights over the second-floor windows could warm those rooms. Some form of shading, such as canvas or bamboo shades, would be needed in summer to prevent the porch from becoming too warm, but the height of the space will allow heat to rise and permit fresh breezes to flow through the porch and the house that would otherwise be trapped by a standard-height ceiling.

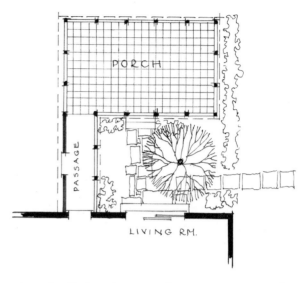

A porch added to a house can often screen out unwanted views of the neighbors' houses.

Screened two-story porches are cooler than one-story structures and shade second-floor windows.

On the North

The north, of course, is the coolest location for a porch. Unless some sunlight is permitted to come in, it can be a rather lifeless location on all but the hottest summer days, and damp and moldy in early spring and late fall. With a one-story house, sunlight is usually no problem. Skylights or a clerestory window across the south side of the new porch addition will extend its use from early spring until late fall. On hot summer days, the clerestory would act as a vent to the high-ceilinged porch, encouraging a breeze that would ventilate the porch and the house as well.

If the house has two stories and would shade a clerestory window, if space permits, you could extend the porch past the corner of the house. If not, the porch could be placed far enough behind the house to get sunlight. Again, you could enclose a small courtyard or terrace accessible from the house and the porch. A covered passage should also be built for use in stormy weather because a porch can be particularly attractive on a muggy summer day.

Since a porch on the north side will get cold winds, you can extend its use by including a few solid walls and some pull-out panels that can be drawn closed to keep out weather and wind. The entire north wall could be solid, and windows could be designed to admit whatever breeze there is in summer.

In designing a porch, never overlook the use of skylights, which can do so much to add character and brighten up an otherwise dull situation. This is especially true of porches on the north because they are in shade so much of the time. The skylights (either glass or plastic) will clean themselves, and are surprisingly easy to install and waterproof.

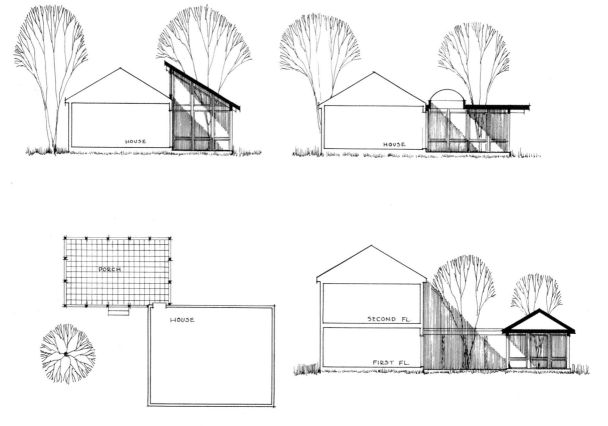

A porch added to the north side of a house can receive sunlight by constructing a clerestory, by offsetting, through use of a skylight, or by completely removing the porch from a two-story structure.

A porch on the east can be protected from the weather with wide overhangs, shutters on the north, and a built-in bench on the south.

On the East

Because of the low level of the rising sun, a porch on the east will not block too much sun from house windows in the morning and will warm up quicker on cool mornings. This makes it the ideal place to have breakfast — if it is off the kitchen. During the summer, the porch will be cooler later in the evening because it will have been shaded by the house a good part of the day. This consideration makes an eastern location a good place for a porch you want to use to relax on after work.

Since an eastern exposure means strong winds in the spring and fall, your use of the porch will be shortened unless you provide some protective walls and planting on the north and east sides. The walls do not need to be structural; they may be simple hinged or sliding panels. Shutters, either operable or nailed in place, could be a quick and attractive solution, since all you need is protection from the wind and slanting rain.

A porch on the east side of the house will have usually cooled off enough to have lunch on the hottest summer days, whereas a porch on the south might be at its warmest by one o'clock in the afternoon. Eastern porches also retain a freshness about them all day in the summer that those in other locations do not, perhaps because all flowers do better with an east light.

If the porch is not too deep, it will not keep sun from kitchen windows and can be appreciated by early risers preparing breakfast. A cool east or northeast porch off the kitchen will also be used and appreciated by anyone who must spend a good amount of time in the kitchen preparing meals and watching youngsters, because children will probably find an east porch the coolest for their summer play. However, a porch on the east will do very little to keep the early morning sun from bedrooms. This can cause consternation if you are a late riser, especially in the summer when you do not want to draw the drapes and shut out the fresh air.

On the West

A porch on the west side of a house will have a magic all its own if it is shaded from the hot afternoon sun on the south. It can be used for viewing sunsets long into the fall of the year. If open on three sides, a west porch will need some protection from fall north winds. This can be an attractive windbreak of evergreens.

Because only a wall or a bank of low evergreens will keep out the long rays of the late afternoon sun, you will not have to be too concerned about blocking out sun from the existing rooms facing west. Tall deciduous trees shading the south and west in summer will help keep the rooms cool during the summer, and in the fall, after these trees have lost their leaves, the sun will warm and light the rooms during the day. You will also be able to use your porch into late November, at least for adult cocktails and a last look at the sunset.

This advantage in the late fall will be a disadvantage during the dog days of August if shading and ventilation are not given top priority. Provide trees, high ceilings, and a roof designed to aid natural circulation, with perhaps an additional ventilating fan in the gable. Even insect screens can keep out some of the breeze, so you might want to use roll-up screening in several panels on each side.

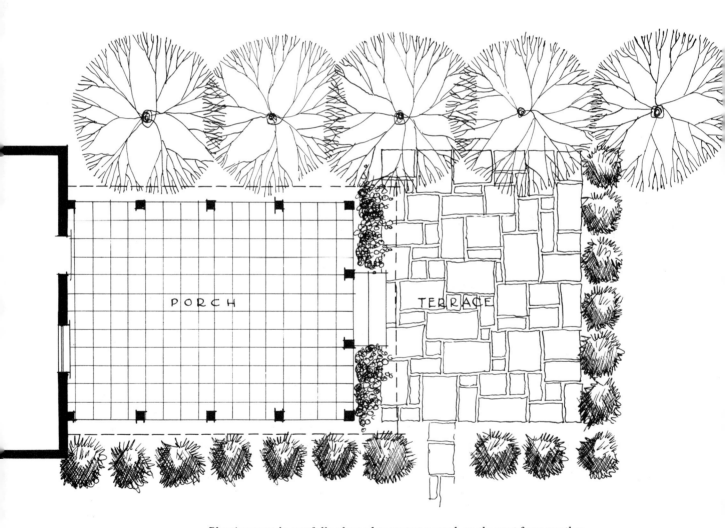

Planting must be carefully planned to protect a porch on the west from weather.

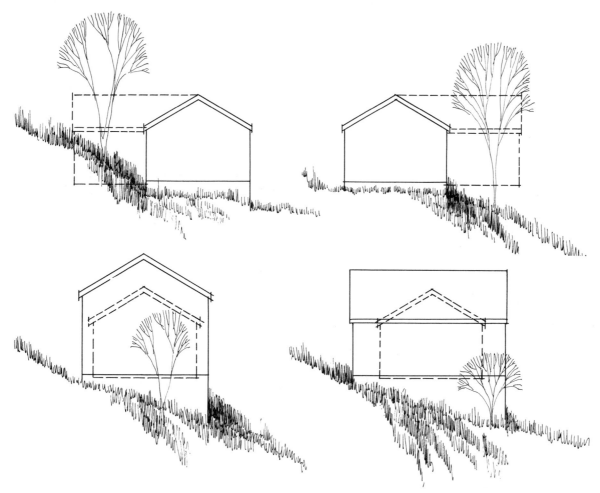

Porches can be designed for difficult sites whether the ground slopes up from the house, away from the house, or intersects the house.

On Difficult Sites

Terraces accommodate themselves to difficult sites much more readily than porches, not only because of their more complicated structure, but also because porch use is more complex. A terrace is an open area connected to the house by steps. A porch is a structure requiring a floor, walls, and roof, and each element must be planned in relation to the floor level, walls, roof, structure, and circulation of the house — plus the architecture and site of the house.

A terrace can be broken into several different areas and be almost a full flight of stairs away from the floor level of the house it is to serve. A porch floor is very nearly the same level as the house, with only enough difference to keep water and melting snow from backing up into the house proper. That is why adding a porch to a house not built on reasonably level ground can present tricky and expensive design problems not always easily solved. To do it well almost always requires some excavating, and if the site is heavily wooded, some trees must be sacrificed. Unlike a wooden deck, you cannot simply leave open spaces for the trees to grow through.

Each situation will be a case unto itself, but some generalities can be assumed. A word should be mentioned concerning the addition of a porch to the typical split-level development house, principally because the majority were built as split-levels only to economize on the depth of the footings and foundation walls; that is, the difference in levels had little or no relation to the site on which they were built. Footings were poured only slightly below grade instead of the usual 3 feet below frost line, then later 3 feet of earth was piled around the foundation to meet the depth requirement of the building code.

On a Slope Up from the House

When the ground slopes up from the house on the side where you would like to add a porch, it can be leveled and graded away from the house and into the hill to create the space required. Basement windows in the porch area should be removed or relocated, and crawl space vents should be moved to another location to assure proper ventilation.

If the slope of the site is not steep, only gentle regrading may be required, providing tree roots and other vegetation can be replanted to retain and stabilize the soil. When the angle of the slope is a lot steeper, one or more low retaining walls may be sufficient to permit the soil to be drained away from the porch location. One of these low walls could perhaps also be used as the foundation for an outside wall of the porch, since it is a structural wall and could act as support for the porch columns and roof. However, if the slope is steep and begins close to the house, regrading and a retaining wall, or a series of smaller retaining walls, will be required to hold back the hillside. Whether the area is subject to slides or not, the structural design of a retaining wall of this extent should only be undertaken by an engineer, and the construction executed under his supervision. Otherwise you may find the pressure of the earth against the wall doing considerable damage to the porch and possibly the house.

Trees, shrubbery, and ground cover should also be replaced to hold the soil and prevent erosion due to quick storms and the runoff of groundwater. This is not meant to discourage you from adding a porch in that location, if that is where it will best suit your home, but only to make you aware of some of the problems you may encounter. It may be preferable to add a terrace there and construct a porch somewhere else. Many times exciting and dramatic solutions are found in overcoming the problems presented by difficult sites.

In many sites of this kind, the view is on the downslope side of the house and the entrance is on the side facing the hill and the street. If you own a two-story house, you may want to add the porch to the second floor and extend the driveway under it to pass in front of the entrance.

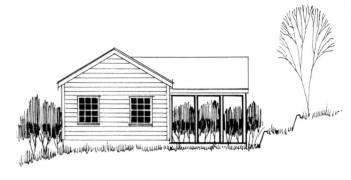

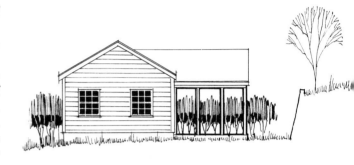

Porches can be added on a slope up from the house by using a series of small retaining walls or one large wall to contain the slope.

Drainage should always be designed to carry the water from the hill and the roof away from the house. This may be simply accomplished by carefully grading the slope, or it may involve burying drain tile in a gravel bed between the slope and the edge of the porch, with the joints covered by building paper and leading to a dry well at one side of the site.

On a Slope Away from the House

Adding a porch on a side where the grade slopes away from the wall of the house does not present quite so many problems or require such expensive solutions. And since this slope often has the best view, it is a logical location for the porch.

A porch may be added to a one-story house built on a crawl space by building a retaining wall, with footings below the frost line on the exterior perimeter of the porch area, and filling it in to provide a solid base for the concrete floor. In some cases, frame construction could be used, but too often this leaves small inaccessible spaces between the porch floor and grade, which may attract stray animals and insects. Unless vents in the crawl space are relocated (*not* covered up), the crawl space will be inadequately ventilated, which could cause dampness.

On a very steep slope, steel Lally columns may be set on individual footings with the floor joist spanning the distance from the foundation wall to a beam supported by the Lally columns. A certain savings may be made in the height of the columns and the depth of the joist by positioning the columns and beam several feet closer to the house and cantilevering the porch over the end of the beam, but these spacings should be checked by an engineer or architect before construction is started. The area under any wooden floor should be kept cleared of brush, dry grass, and evergreens so there is no chance of a ground fire spreading under the frame construction.

Homes built on full basements can take advantage of a first-floor porch to make a covered terrace or porch off the basement on a steep slope by a little extra grading and the reinforcement of the basement footing in that area. The space might also be used as a carport, since it will provide some weather protection for an automobile, but areas under open porches should not be enclosed because the wood floors are not tight and will not be waterproof. A built-up roof with a floor finish of slate or tile could be made if the area under the porch is to be used to extend the basement for a garage or a usable room in the basement.

When the grade is such that you do not want to excavate for a basement terrace, you can build steps down from the house to the porch floor. The roof line of the porch should be retained at the plate line of the house to maintain the view, light, and circulation of air in the existing house. This can create quite an interesting story-and-a-half porch. Additional sunlight can be let in by opening the gable end of the porch. Extra-large overhangs of 4 feet should be used on the porch so that it is well protected from rain.

If the view offers no attraction and it is a real cost savings to continue the roof line down to a lower level to protect the porch, to let sunlight into windows covered by the roof of the new

Porches can be added on a slope away from the house with the use of a retaining wall or by excavating the basement area.

porch, run a skylight the entire length of the roof at its intersection with the house wall. The skylight should be a ventilating type to prevent the buildup of heat, which, would cause the house to overheat in the summer. But the skylight will help to heat it during the winter months.

A combination of skylights and a flat roof on the porch could also be used if ventilation, view, and sunlight are equally desired, or if a flat roof is preferred to coordinate the design of the porch with that of the house.

On an Intersecting Slope

Too often when the grade intersects the location desired for a porch, we take the easy way out and strike a balance somewhere in the middle. Unfortunately, this does not always produce the least expensive or the most attractive porch. A porch on an intersecting slope is possible where the garage is in the basement of the house and a full flight of exterior steps is needed to get to the front door, or where there is a legitimate reason (because of the slope of the property) for having one area of the house on one level and another area a few steps up or down.

Some very interesting results can be obtained by carefully studying the levels and designing the porch in combination with a terrace or enclosed construction so that together they create a new aspect of the house. A part of the new porch, for instance, could enclose an entrance hall and stairs so that you can get from the driveway into the house on the same level. The intersection might be at a place where you could add a porch on two levels and at the same time gain inexpensive storage space in the basement. Or perhaps a low-level terrace could be combined with a porch at a higher level, either one of which by itself might be a bit dull, but which in combination add interest to each.

Each case is so individual that generalities in this area are not advisable. Perhaps the illustrations will give you enough ideas as to what can be done that your imagination will be spurred to think of possibilities that would work with your own house.

Porches added on intersecting slopes present a challenge to imaginative design but often inspire very interesting solutions.

8
The Best Porch in the Right Place

A porch can be so much more than just a roofed platform with screening tacked around it to keep the bugs out and a steel-sprung screen door that is constantly banging as the youngsters run in and out. A well-placed and carefully planned porch can be the center of family life for almost half the year — from May to October. Even longer, if it is designed with wide overhangs to keep out the rain and hot summer sun and provide shelter from spring and fall winds, and perhaps heated. (Why not include a fireplace, or a Franklin or potbelly stove?) Chances are you have a living room fireplace that is used only three months out of the year, between Thanksgiving and Valentine's Day. On many nights you would enjoy an open fire on a porch to take the chill off, or just to add cheer. You could also use a fireplace or stove for cooking, which can be a joy on a wet summer evening.

A terrace does not have to be right up against the house (it is usually a mistake if it is), but a porch must have at least one wall in common with the house. Before you go the expense of constructing a porch, you may want to build a terrace in the location you have chosen to see how outdoor living will affect the circulation in the house, how much you actually use the new addition, if it is the right size, if the placement is the best for view, sunlight, privacy, breeze, and drainage. Would a roof and screened walls really improve its usefulness enough to warrant the added expense? If you are not sure at the outset, the terrace will help you decide. If it is designed to carry the weight of walls and a roof, it can be made into a porch after you are absolutely sure of the location.

Many people build porch additions to their homes and enjoy them so much that they wish to use them the whole year. So have them glassed in and enclosed, only to find that the original enchantment is lost. What was once a delightful summertime area becomes a heated, air-conditioned, curtained, and carpeted room of no set purpose and very little distinction. No one knows where the living room (or dining room) ends and the porch begins, and neither room does a thing for the other in terms of usefulness and comfort. A porch can too easily become a part of the room adjoining it. It is important for each to keep a separate identity or the change in atmosphere is lost.

Entrance Porch

It used to be, in the old days, that almost every house had a wide and welcoming front porch. Not, of course, in the very old days. The first settlers, even if they had known what a front porch was (and they did not) would have been afraid to use it for sitting. And porches were certainly not used during the Georgian era, when more stately houses had protective porticos at the entrance (hardly the place to set out an old glider and a rocking chair). No, it was not until the more openhearted Italians and other Mediterranean immigrants arrived here and Americans began to travel abroad that the front porch began to be built. It was during the nineteenth century, when England was still an empire and the British began to

Simply remodeling the entrance porch and changing the front door give added character and dignity to an entrance.

Architect, A. J. Harmon, A.I.A.

Frank Russell

The house before the porch was added.

The architect's rendering shows how the house will look after the porch has been added. Architect, A. J. Harmon, A.I.A.

This house was transformed by adding an entrance porch and a new window. The porch, accessible from kitchen and living room, has a solid front wall giving it privacy from the street and is open to the garden on two sides.

call their one-story houses bungalows (an Anglo-Indian word meaning, literally, belonging to Bengal) and added verandas (Hindu for porch), that many Americans began tacking porches on to classic Georgian and Early American houses. A Victorian house could scarcely be built in this country without a big front porch or veranda, and they continued to be built and added on until World War I. Ladies would sit, surrounded by green lawns, and nod greetings to their friends and neighbors strolling by and frown as the noise from a horseless carriage shattered the quiet summer afternoon.

After the war, everyone got too sophisticated and busy voting and the like to enjoy leisurely teas. And no one wanted to sit on a porch smothered by the dust, fumes, and noise from

The garden side of this small house before and after the addition of the entrance porch.

the passing traffic anyway. Now we have come full circle; like the early colonists, we have no idea who might be lurking just beyond the foundation planting.

The front porch today is a relatively small, paved, covered, well-lighted space that protects the front door and guests from the weather. It seldom functions as well as the old porte cochere (a French word meaning coach door), which has degenerated into our carport that usually leads to a back door.

The ideal entrance porch should be on the driveway. If this is not possible, it should be clearly visible and easily accessible from the drive — not up steps, around corners, and past bedroom, dining room, or living room windows. The absolute minimum size is 5 feet square. Most entrance doors are 3 feet wide, which allows only a foot of free space on either side of the door. Front doors swing in, but since many have screen or storm doors that swing out, the 5-foot minimum allows only 2 feet for a guest to stand on while the door is being opened.

Entrance platforms higher than a foot should have a railing. All steps should be lighted, and you should never have a single step except at a threshold, where it is expected. A small step 6 inches high should be broken down into two 3-inch steps, which are more obvious and safer. Any run of more than three steps should be provided with a handrail, and if they ascend to the entrance porch, should not be located where rain or snow runoff can turn to ice.

Lighting at the entrance door should be at eye level and there should be one light on either side of the door so you will have a clear view of the face of anyone at the door before you open it. Lights that are mounted too high or in the ceiling will cast a person's face in shadow and you will not be able to see them clearly.

If you live in a suburban area, provide an old-fashioned mud scraper at the side of the entrance so snow and mud can be scraped off shoes and boots. For year round use, a hemp doormat (not a plastic one) can be set in the floor in front of the door so it will not be blown away or tripped over. It comes in standard sizes, so replacement is no problem, and it can be removed easily for cleaning.

Living Room Porch

If the porch is attached to the living room, it will be used in the warm months very much as the living room is used in winter. If yours is a formal living room, with precise furniture groupings for conversation aimed more at the convenience of adults than younger people, the porch will tend to be used in the same way in the summer, with classical music from the living room drifting out into the fresh air. If your living room is informal and used by both children and adults, the record player and television set will probably be moved out in warm weather, along with the bridge table and portable bar. The success or failure of either type of porch will depend on its privacy from the street and whether it is accessible from another room besides the living room; in the case of the formal living room, it would be from an entrance hall, and in the case of an informal living room, from the kitchen. Either should have access to the garden, and preferably a terrace off the porch, so that on warm evenings when everyone wants to be outdoors they do not have to huddle together in the same space.

Every porch other than an entrance porch, should be screened or designed so that it can be screened in the future. The columns and supports for the roof should be spaced so that standard screening fits between them (insect screen comes in rolls with widths of from 24 to 48 inches).

A railing should be used on all porches, whether there is danger of anyone falling off or not, to warn people, especially tots, that the

A living room porch added to the front of the house can have privacy from the street by adding a solid, but windowed, front wall.

open space is not a door and may have screen across it. A railing will also prevent careless people from shoving the back of a chair or table against or through the screen. But a railing can be most annoying if not placed at the right height from the floor. Too many times it is placed so that when you are sitting down it is exactly at eye level and you are forced to either look over or under it. Before you establish the height of the railing (and sometimes minimum heights are regulated by the building code for safety), sit in a chair that you will be using on the porch to check if you have to strain your neck to see over, or duck your head to see under, the railing. It may seem a small thing at the time, but such a test can avoid years of ducking and straining.

Since the porch is to be off the living room,

we shall assume that it will combine the functions of the living room with outdoor recreation activities, that it will be used on quiet evenings and long summer weekends. The porch should have a separate entrance from a terrace or garden, one from the kitchen if possible, and one from the living room or entrance hall. You may want to have access from the living room, but this is not always essential. In fact, in many ways, it is better if the living room can be kept separate from the porch — providing you can create an entrance to the porch from an entrance hall. This will double the life of the living room carpet, drapes, and furniture.

It is also a distinct advantage not to have the living room windows darkened by the porch. This may not be serious in the case of a formal living room that is not used much during the

A glass or plastic roof on a porch opens it to sunlight and air while solid walls on one or more sides retain privacy and security.

day, but it is important if the living room is a gathering place for the family during the winter, when you will want it warmed and brightened by the sun.

A porch off the living room should be as large, if not larger than, the living room itself since it is not advisable to have furniture lined up around the walls because without adequate overhangs it can get soaked in a sudden shower. Lining the walls with furniture in a living room proper is never a good idea either, though sometimes in a small living room there is no other way to place the furniture. However, on a porch, you may have only one, or two, protected walls, and the further you can keep lounges, chairs, and tables from the screened outside walls, the better use you can make of the porch.

Entertaining and serving family snacks and light summer suppers are easier if the porch connects to the kitchen. This is not always an easy matter to arrange, but it sometimes can be accomplished by carefully juggling the design and even by placing the porch in, what seems at first an incongruous location — such as opposite the kitchen — and then connecting it and the kitchen with a loggia.

There should be a light over every threshold and over all steps. Convenience outlets should be placed in the one or two house walls, where there is no danger of coming into contact with wet wiring. All outlets should be of the exterior kind approved by the Board of Fire Underwriters. It is best to avoid table lamps because they may be blown over in a storm. Where reading lights are desired, fasten them to the house

A porch removed from the main part of the house may still be connected to the kitchen by the use of a loggia.

wall and control them with interior switches.

If you want an outdoor grill on the porch, put it where there will be some solid wall around it and where it will be out of strong winds in early spring and late fall. If the porch backs up on a fireplace on an interior wall, this may be the ideal location for a Franklin stove. Expose as much flue as you can because that is where a great deal of the heat is generated. An iron

A cupola on the roof of the porch greatly increases air circulation.

stove such as a Franklin or potbelly stove will have to be protected in the winter with a coat of oil to keep it from rusting, but the effort is small compared to the amount of pleasure the fire and warmth will give you.

It is also a good idea to include a freezeproof hose bib on the porch, not only for fire protection, but also for cleaning up in the spring and fall. You will be surprised at the amount of sand and dirt that will filter through a straw mat rug in one summer. The walls, too, will need to be cleaned — not only the screens, but also the interior house walls. House paint is manufactured so that through the action of rain it cleans itself, but the walls covered by the porch roof cannot benefit from this natural cleaning and, depending on the area in which you live, the difference may be quite noticeable every year or so. Also, a hose bib on the porch will make it much easier to water the potted plants that you are sure to collect for display there.

Furniture storage will have to be considered. If your porch furniture is painted wrought iron or aluminum, or even wood, the larger and bulkier pieces may be left out all winter, but small tables, glass tops, cushions, and accessories should be put away. A good-sized closet can usually be fitted into a space against the house wall for convenient winter storage; in the summer, it can be used for umbrellas, extra plastic glasses and trays, and accessories for a terrace that may be next to the porch.

While you are adding the porch, be sure to have any solid walls and the roof insulated against the day when you might decide to make the porch into a year-round room.

If you are adding a one-story porch to a two-story house, you should consider making the roof into a second-floor terrace or a sun deck off the bedrooms. It will cost more because flat roofs require stronger joists to carry the live and snow loads, but a second-floor terrace is very pleasant, especially at night or to relax on alone. It is also excellent for elderly people who may not want to make the trip downstairs to sit in the sun and enjoy the fresh air, especially if they have their own private porch away from the noisier activities of the house and youngsters.

Dining Room Porch

If you decide on a porch off the dining room, usually it is because you want to enjoy your meals there most of the summer. A porch is more advantageous than a terrace because you can dine on it rain or shine. You will probably want a dining table and chairs in a permanent location, plus seating and lounge space for relaxing, cocktails, entertaining, and casual preparation of summertime lunches and dinners.

A built-in fireplace and grill, either one of masonry that uses charcoal or a manufactured gas or electric grill, will allow you to cook on the porch in the presence of your family and guests. The masonry fireplace and grill will be more expensive initially, but cheaper to operate, and since it can also be used for warmth, it will extend the use of the porch from early spring into late fall.

Of course, privacy and security, insect screening, interior circulation, and the effect the porch will have on light and air in the rooms inside must all be considered before you add a dining room (or any) porch.

It is essential that a dining room porch be directly accessible from the kitchen, with as few steps between them, horizontally and vertically, as possible. Storage for cookware, dishes, and glassware on the porch makes little difference because you will have to take them into the kitchen for washing. However, you will want storage for lounge and sofa cushions. The dining chairs will probably have removable seat cushions, so these can also be stored in winter, along with table accessories, paper napkins, hurricane lamps and candles, which will provide the best and most romantic lighting for both dining and relaxing.

Other lighting should be provided for cleaning and security. Garden lighting will attract insects away from the screens and provide pleasant illumination of green foliage at night, but it should be of low wattage and aimed at medium-height shrubbery, not taller trees, so it does not shine into a neighbor's bedroom.

A telephone jack is also a handy thing to have on a dining porch because you will be spending a lot of time there. Also, if you happen to be working in the garden, you will not have to run into the house to answer it.

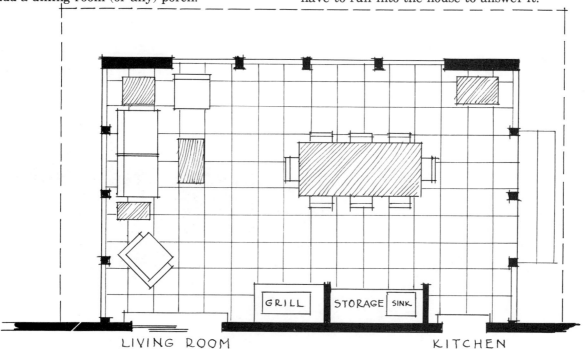

A dining room porch should have access from the kitchen as well as from the living room or dining room.

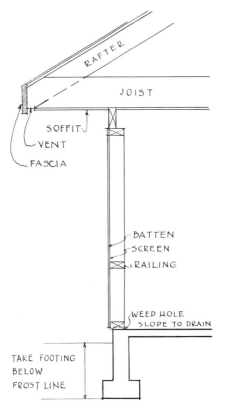

RAFTER

JOIST

SOFFIT

VENT

FASCIA

BATTEN

SCREEN

RAILING

WEEP HOLE
SLOPE TO DRAIN

TAKE FOOTING
BELOW
FROST LINE

Section through a porch wall and roof.

A hose bib should be provided for quick hosing down several times a week to keep food crumbs from attracting insects, and screened weep holes every 4 feet at the bottom of the exterior walls will allow the water to run off without backing up. A wet sink with a cold-water tap for rinsing dishes, would also be a good idea, but it is not essential.

Hemp or straw rugs should not be used under the table because the chair legs will tear them apart in a short time, and if they happen to get wet from a shower, they will take a long time to dry out. Indoor-outdoor carpet can be used if you think you must have something to cover the floor, but usually the bare floor is a lot cooler looking and more attractive.

If you choose a glass-top dining table, do not get clear plate glass unless you do not mind looking at people's feet all through dinner. An opaque or obscure glass is easier to keep clean and much more satisfactory.

A hanging electric lighting fixture over the table will be blown by the wind, and if the table is removed and stored in the winter (as it should be), there is a chance that someone could injure himself by walking into the hanging fixture.

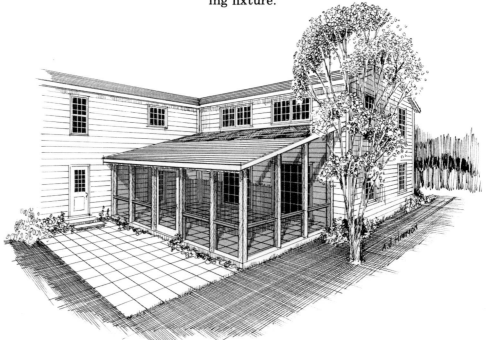

A glass or plastic skylight on the porch roof permits sunlight to enter windows which would otherwise be shaded.

Family Room Porch

It is usually assumed that a porch built off a family room is going to be large, informal, close to the kitchen, and that it will lead directly to the backyard and the children's play area. As is almost always the case, a terrace and a porch can work together here to improve the usefulness of both. The terrace can be used as a place for the children to play during the day, while the adults in the family relax in the shade of the porch, still maintaining close supervision of the youngsters. At night, the children will probably be more interested in summer reruns on television than a starry vista and a fresh clean breeze.

A terrace will also help keep the porch cleaner and tidier. It will absorb the rough play, roller skating, basketball games, and the mud, grass, and sand that might normally be tracked into the house through the porch. And if you have a porch just off the terrace, the "what will we do if it rains?" problem will not be quite so severe when you have invited a lot of relatives over for a barbecue. The porch should be of a good size, with wide overhangs to keep out the rain during family outings and to shelter children as they ride tricycles and play hopscotch on rainy afternoons. On or between the porch and the family room should be a storage closet large enough to stash summer outdoor games, the badminton set, croquet mallets and balls, a portable sandbox, beach balls, a folding Ping-Pong table, seat cushions, and porch and terrace accessories such as hurricane lamps and candles.

You will probably not want a gas or electric grill on the porch if there are small children in

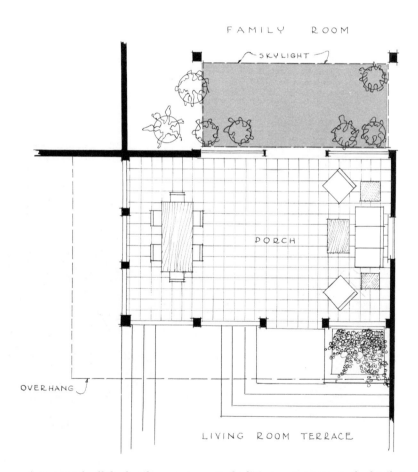

FAMILY ROOM

SKYLIGHT

PORCH

OVERHANG

LIVING ROOM TERRACE

A new porch off the family room connects the living room terrace to the family room.

Before the new porch was added (see plan, p. 59), the family room was separated from the living room and the rest of the house.

The openness of the new porch, separated from the family room by a skylight, is a pleasant addition to the living room terrace.   *Architect, A. J. Harmon, A.I.A.*

Frank Russell

the family — especially gas, since the detection of an open burner is difficult outdoors. Even a masonry fireplace and grill may not be worth the expense with the kitchen so close by. However pleasant an open fire on the porch may be, with active youngsters playing on the floor, bouncing balls, and creating confusion, a fireplace and grill may not be advisable. Picnickers forced off the terrace by bad weather can adjourn to the porch and family room.

Because of its proximity to the kitchen, the family room porch will almost inevitably be used as a dining area. Probably you will not need a large sit-down dining table; individual trays are enough. A combination water fountain, wet bar, and hose bib would be a good addition to a family room porch. It can quench little thirsts quickly and is also a good place for flower arranging, watering potted plants, and, by attaching a hose, cleaning up floors, screens, and walls — which will make housekeeping easier on a much-used porch.

Lighting should be kept simple, with perhaps one flush ceiling light for security.

The skylight separating the porch from the family room allows additional sunlight into the room where plants and orange trees bloom all winter.   Architect, A. J. Harmon, A.I.A.

Frank Russell

The Best Porch in the Right Place   61

Plastic skylights can be set in flat or sloping roofs. The protective paper should not be removed until all other work is completed because the plastic is easily scratched.

Plate glass skylight on a sloping roof can be sealed and waterproofed with new silicone.

Children will not be using the porch after dark for study and a few candles are usually preferred by adults for a more relaxing atmosphere. There should be several waterproof electric outlets for a television set, record player, and radio.

If the addition of a porch is going to darken the family room, consider using a more unconventional roof design or skylights so that the all-important winter sun is not shut out. On a traditional house, skylights can be combined with unobtrusive flat roofs to permit the kind of adaptable solution that is usually the least expensive because of ease of construction and minimum of flashing. Open gables and clerestory windows are another way of admitting light into darkened family rooms, though these are not always adaptable to standard 8-foot-high ceilings.

Kitchen Porch

A porch off the kitchen used to have a variety of uses. Actually half-pantry and half-open porch, it housed the icebox, which used real 100-pound blocks of ice delivered several times a week in the summer, and storage bins for vegetables, wood, and coal. Many times there was a big old coal stove on the open porch that was used in the summer for canning the vegetables that would be stored first in the basement and then in the pantry, to be eaten all winter in an age without supermarkets. The porch was usually on the north or east side of the house, where it would be as cool as possible. Every afternoon in late summer and fall, great pots of fruits and vegetables that were being "put up" simmered quietly until they were ready to be ladled into Mason jars and lined neatly on dark basement shelves.

Kitchen porches are still more utilitarian than decorative, but now that the refrigerator is in the kitchen and not as many people can as used to, the porch may be much smaller. A kitchen porch can still be put to excellent use, however, and remains better located on the north or east side of the house as a cool retreat for a midmorning cup of coffee or a noontime lunch.

You may decide to imbed the garbage cans in the floor of the porch, but it is actually better to put them further away on the other side of the driveway or garage to keep flies and other insects away from a place you use for relaxation.

A hose bib is most essential on a kitchen porch, and if you have a vegetable garden (as so many people do these days), a sink with a cold-water faucet will be very useful for rinsing your hands and washing garden vegetables. A small potting bench and a counter for flower

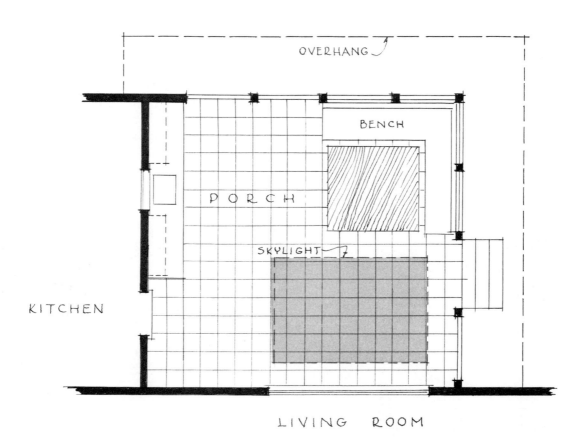

Skylight placed over living room window on kitchen porch adds extra light to the porch and permits sunlight to enter living room.

arranging would also be useful and decorative on a kitchen porch.

A standard kitchen counter top will not hold up outdoors, but tile or slate will, and both can easily be put down by amateur craftsmen. A sheet of stainless steel or aluminum could be nailed over the counter for all-weather protection, and cleans up easily. Any chemicals or fertilizer could be stored in a wall or base cabinet, but keep the doors locked to protect children and pets. Metal cabinets will rust outdoors, so use sturdy wood cabinets that you can put together yourself.

A small table and a few chairs will probably be the only furniture required, or you could build a bench along an outside wall instead of a railing. Keep the overhangs wide so you can use the bench when it is raining without having to worry about the cushions and table getting wet.

A minimum of electricity will be needed since it is unlikely that you will use the porch at night. Any steps should be lighted and there should also be a light by the back door that is controlled by a three-way switch — one in the kitchen and another in the garage, so you can turn the light on and off when you arrive home after dark or want to take the garbage out at night.

It is important not to darken the kitchen windows with a porch roof. If this is going to be a problem, perhaps you should consider making the porch roof partially of glass or translucent plastic. Silicone rubber waterproofing compounds, while expensive, make glass and plastic inserts in roofs so easy to work with

Kitchen porch with a skylight (see plan, p. 63) has a built-in bench and table for eating and a cold-water sink for washing garden vegetables and arranging flowers.

that even an inexperienced homeowner will have little trouble.

Garage Porch

Perhaps off the garage is not the usual place for a porch, but it should be considered because so many of the projects we set aside for doing in the summer are messy and a garage porch makes an excellent outdoor summer workshop. The garage itself might be a good enough place to paint lawn furniture, build cabinets, and store wood, but even if the car is left in the driveway, it will get covered with sawdust and speckled with paint, and the oil on the garage floor will inevitably get transferred to the chest of drawers you have just painted white.

A porch off the garage has the advantage of being away from the house. It is quiet, removed, a good place to relax away from the television and the telephone. It can be as deep as you want, and you do not have to worry about blocking out light or air from any rooms in your house. You can make as much noise there as you wish without disturbing anyone who might be sleeping. If you like to work early in the morning or late at night, you can saw and hammer to your heart's content. Since the walls are open (though perhaps screened), you can paint and varnish without having to worry about proper ventilation, and things can dry properly there without being moved or brushed against.

The garage will probably already have some electricity and it can be extended to the porch to light a workbench or provide power for several reading lights and a television for Saturday and Sunday afternoon sports programs. You might also want to put the old refrigerator there when you buy a new one for the kitchen so you can enjoy a cold beer, and the children can have soft drinks. (It will also be handy for extra ice cubes for a neighborhood party.)

A cold-water line can easily be run from the house for cleaning paintbrushes and scrubbing up. It does not have to drain into a septic tank or sewer, but can empty into a simple dry well you can dig and connect yourself.

Paint stored there will have to be moved in the winter because it cannot be allowed to freeze, which is also true of most stains and

A garage porch, added either to the side or the back, can be a quiet retreat or workshop.

varnishes. However, since painting supplies kept more than a year tend to disintegrate and change color, there may be no advantage to saving them anyway.

Winter use would include a storage place for snow-shoveling and ice-melting equipment for the driveway, sleds, skiis, and other winter sports gear. Firewood and kindling could also be stored on the garage porch, so you will not have to worry about termites and other wood-destroying insects getting into the house.

Bedroom Porch

Before the days of effective central heating and air conditioning, hardy Bernard MacFadden types had sleeping porches off their bedrooms. Winter and summer, they would bundle up in woolens and nightcaps to sleep in the open air — a practice that was thought to, if not cure, at least avert any number of illnesses. Women, at that time the weaker sex, were usually excluded from such folly and were permitted to remain indoors and forego the healthful aspects of the freezing cold night air and the specious pleasure of waking up under a light blanket of snow (though some old-fashioned sleeping porches were glassed in for protection from the snow and rain in those days before vinyl and waterproof sleeping bags). In winter, the inadequately heated house seemed almost overheated in comparison, but in summer, the sleeping porch was usually cooler and more comfortable than the heavily draped bedrooms.

Today a porch off a bedroom, especially one on the first floor, would not be used for sleeping, but it would be a nice, quiet retreat where your mind could turn to pleasant thoughts after a day of wrestling with problems. The roof of the porch will protect the bedroom doors, so that once you go to sleep, you will be able to enjoy sudden summer showers without having to jump up and close the doors to prevent the rain from soaking the carpet, drapes, and furniture. The usefulness of the porch will be increased if the bedroom area is also protected by a walled courtyard for privacy and security. In this instance, a screened bedroom porch could be designed almost as a summer bedroom, with bamboo shades, canvas drapes, or vine-covered trellises to keep out drafts and the early morning sun. Lightweight sleeping bags could be placed over canvas- or vinyl-covered polyethylene mattresses on bed-sized benches at night and folded and stored in a closet during the day.

Two-story houses give you the advantage of

A bedroom porch surrounded by a garden wall for security. Canvas drapes close to keep out drafts and rain.

security. A sleeping porch, or even a small balcony for relaxation, could be built for sunbathing, quiet reading, and letter writing. The bedroom itself will buffer household noises. If there is an enclosed porch under the bedroom porch, the floor of the bedroom porch will have to be waterproofed. This can be done in several ways, but probably the easiest and least expensive is to apply a built-up roof and then, using duckboards, build a second wearable floor for the porch. Tile, slate, or brick could be used, but the weight of these materials will require heavier than usual joists.

Bedroom and sleeping porches usually have solid railings for additional privacy, although these will cut down on the air circulation. A series of window boxes mounted on top of the railing and planted with quick-growing annuals and trailing vines such as morning glories will allow the breeze to come through and add a little height to the screening.

An inexpensive and quite usable second-floor porch, either roofed or open, could be built by using Lally columns to support a deck. The floor would not have to be waterproofed if there is no enclosed porch under it. Screening and a roof will double the porch's use and, for sleeping out, the space between the planks will allow air circulation and create a cooling effect on warm nights.

Electricity should be handled very carefully on any porch that is not completely enclosed and waterproof. Reading lights may be used if they are permanently mounted on the wall and controlled with a waterproof switch. Electric blankets should not be permitted on an open or screened sleeping porch. They are not designed for exterior use, and any contact with dampness could start a fire or result in serious shock.

For heat on a bedroom porch, use a well-protected Franklin stove. The placement should be carefully planned so that a breeze will not make it smoke up the porch, and it should be at least 6 feet away from any beds or camping equipment used for sleeping.

If you plan to have large pots of plants and flowers on the porch, a hose bib will save you many trips back and forth from the bathroom with a pitcher to water them. For a sleeping porch, you might want to consider an exterior telephone jack for late night calls or leisurely Saturday morning conversation with friends.

Bedroom porch on the second floor is secluded and private among the treetops. Shades roll down to control wind and rain.

Basement Porch

Unlike a terrace, a porch off the basement may not be a good idea unless the house is built on a hill and most of the basement is exposed to fresh circulating air. Otherwise the roof of the basement porch will retain dampness, making the basement and the rest of the house damp. The porch roof would also keep sunlight out of the basement (one of the prime reasons for having the basement wall exposed). Enclosing the basement area with a retaining wall and then adding a roof to part of it could create an uncomfortable pressure-cooker effect.

However, if the site slopes sharply away from the basement and you are adding a porch on the first floor, a basement porch could be considered, especially one in the form of a sun porch that is entirely open to the basement. It would preferably be on the south side of the house, with a light-reflecting terrace surround-ing it to give you additional light in the basement and to drain water and moisture away.

If the basement porch is glass-enclosed, the floor of the porch above must be waterproofed. If you do not want to go to this expense, a floor with slightly larger spaces between the planks will let more air circulate up through the floor and will help eliminate heat and dampness. Any additional height you can gain by sinking the floor of the basement porch will also aid air circulation and the problem of buildup of damp air under the first-floor porch.

Water from the roofs will have to be carefully drained off with gutters and downspouts to dry wells or runoffs farther down the hill. Trees should be placed to shade the first-floor porch, though not the basement porch, because you will want the sun to dispel as much moisture as possible. Foundation planting around the basement should also be kept low to allow air to circulate freely around the walls and through the floor.

9
Flooring and Roofs

After location and design, the floor of a porch or terrace is the basis for its success or failure. The most important factors are suitability, appearance, durability, and drainage, and probably the most crucial is drainage. If water puddles form in the center of the floor or the surrounding earth washes over the floor with every rain, the terrace or porch will become more of a chore than a pleasure. Water will be constantly tracked into the house from the puddles, and soil washed over the most carefully designed floor will look very disagreeable and sloppy, especially on a terrace where the only demarkation line is the crisp green of ground cover. Apart from being unsightly in summer, bad drainage can be a serious and dangerous problem in winter when ice forms in unpredictable spots. Moisture may freeze in small, once imperceptible masonry cracks, and as the ice expands the cracks will become wider. The next time more water gets in, it will expand that much more, and so on, until it becomes a maintenance problem.

Deterioration of a terrace floor because of poor drainage and an insufficient base can be an annoyance, but on a porch floor the consequences are much more serious. A structural failure in a porch floor can cause the walls to change position and allow the roof to sag.

After proper grading and, depending on soil conditions, after the sub-base has been established, a terrace can be built very quickly and inexpensively. If you believe that someday you will want to add a porch in that location, it may be better to construct the terrace floor as a structural base, carrying the footings 3 feet below grade, so that porch columns and a roof can be added at a later time with no alterations and no loss of time or materials.

Terrace Floors

Gravel Terrace: A gravel terrace is the quickest, least expensive terrace to put down. It will require some maintenance from time to time as weeds may grow through it. Wear, traffic, and snow shoveling tend to dissipate it, so every several years some new gravel will have to be added. To minimize washed-out areas, the terrace can be divided into smaller sections with brick or strips of treated wood. Edging with header boards wherever the gravel meets a planting area or lawn will keep the gravel from disappearing into the grass.

A bed of crushed rock under the gravel will help hold the surface and steady the edges. The gravel should not be deeper than 1½ inches, or it will be uncomfortable to walk on. Gravel of much less depth, or gravel laid directly on soil without a crushed rock base, will soon show soil and mud on its surface. To prevent weeds from growing through, but still allow the gravel to wash itself and not become waterlogged, place 2- or 3-foot strips of overlapping plastic under the gravel. Be very sure that the plastic is placed on a flat surface and tamped down, with the gravel covering it evenly so small ends of the plastic do not surface. Do not use a single large piece of plastic, as it would not permit water to drain through lapped strips. Although in warm weather the water would probably drain off to the sides eventually, in the winter it could freeze and become slippery.

You can buy gravel in different colors, and if the terrace is used more for ornamental purposes, such as a setting for a fountain or a sundial and a foreground for an azalea garden, alternate squares could be filled in with lighter and darker gravel. However, if the terrace is to be actively used, it is not worth the effort and extra expense because the colors will soon be kicked from one square to the next.

Gravel is sold in different sizes that vary from fine to very coarse. Avoid the fine pea gravel because it constantly shifts and is carried into grass areas and the house, as it sticks to shoes and bare feet. Since the large sizes are hard to walk on, it is better to use medium-size gravel that will give you a firm footing but will not be easily tracked about.

Of course, this underfoot feeling of gravel is one of its biggest drawbacks. Women tend to hate it because the heels of their shoes often sink in, making it very difficult to walk, and gravel finding its way between feet and sandals can be painful. Sharp coarse gravel can be very painful on bare feet, and river-washed or rounded gravel, unless medium sized and uniform, can cause stone bruises. All gravels make it necessary to lay a strip of lawn or doormat between the terrace and the house to keep the gravel from being tracked inside.

Gravel terraces are for adults only. While it

A simple gravel terrace is the least expensive to build and allows trees to grow through it for shade.

A sod terrace should be well drained, and separated from other lawn area by aluminum or treated wood edging.

is relatively soft and children will not be hurt in falls, the youngest ones tend to eat it. And usually older children are simply too active for it, making holes in it and spreading it around from terrace to garden to house.

The main advantages of gravel for a terrace are that it cleans itself, is quick and easy to lay in an afternoon, and is inexpensive. Very little maintenance is required, and with just a little care, it provides a clean, cool, and very attractive surface that dries quickly after a shower.

Sod Terrace: We do not usually think of grass as a terrace flooring material, but it should be considered because it has some interesting aspects. It, too, should be sloped to drain quickly so mud does not form, but it needs no other base than the existing soil. Edging should be provided around the outside to separate the sod from the lawn, as they may be different kinds of grasses requiring different treatment.

The terrace area can be designed in any shape and may have several different levels. The stairs may be made of sod, too, simply by

boxing out with treated wood, filling with soil, and fitting the cut sod into the area. Several days of light to medium watering will be required before the joints completely disappear, but if need be, the sod terrace could be used as soon as it is finished if it is watered immediately after.

There are many different kinds of sod available. You should get the heartiest that will grow in your area. Sod is usually sold in 1-foot-wide strips 2 or 3 feet long. It is well to have the terrace area prepared before the sod is delivered so it can be placed without delay, although it may be kept stacked in neat rows not more than 2 feet high for a day or two if the weather is not too damp. The sod will be 2 to 3 inches thick, depending on the root length and the soil in which it is planted.

To lay the sod, begin with the outside edging and do a length about a yard wide. Pound it down firmly with a block or wide wooden board on a handle. Do not walk on the surface until it has been pounded down. Work your way around all the edges toward the center, taking

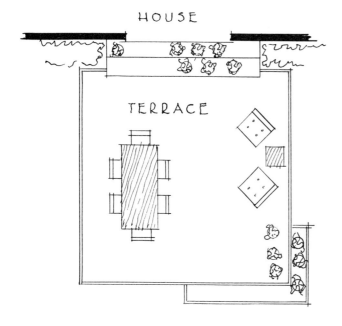

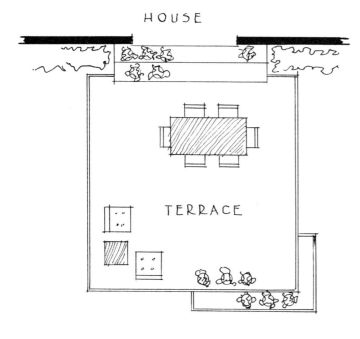

The furniture arrangement on a sod terrace should be changed, and potted plants used to alternate traffic patterns.

off uneven pieces of dirt from the back or from the sides to assure a very tight fit. Water well the first few days. After that, it can be treated very much like regular grass.

A sod terrace can be exceptionally effective where the soil around the house is not conducive to growing grass, where there is a lot of sand and sun, or where a good lawn refuses to grow because of the abundance of trees, rocks, and ground cover. Aside from being almost instantaneous, a sod terrace is soft, glareless, and quiet. It will not reflect the heat from the sun or noise from the surrounding area. Toddlers may get grass-stained from falling down, but what is that compared to scraped knees and elbows?

Sod is a pleasant surface to walk on and is navigable in the highest heels and flimsiest sandals. But sod, like any grass, will collect dew, which feels invigorating on bare feet, but can ruin shoes. With careful watering, cutting every week, and the application of the proper fertilizer, a sod terrace will stay healthy, lush, and green all summer.

Maintenance is the most difficult problem. While not requiring the expert care of a golf green, like a golf green where the cup must be moved frequently, a sod terrace demands weekly rearrangement of the furniture. Otherwise worn spots and paths will soon show. The entrance from the house and garden needs to be altered slightly every week, and this can be done by simply changing the location of some potted plants to block out one space and open another. Steps, if made wide enough, can be handled in the same way so that worn paths will not appear.

Outdoor furniture should be smaller in scale and lighter in weight than the usual outdoor furniture for easier shifting. Since it must be moved once a week when you cut the grass, it will not be difficult to place it in a different location each time. Because of this necessity to shift furniture, make a sod terrace at least a third larger than a terrace with a more durable flooring surface.

Masonry Terraces: A number of masonry materials can be set in sand to make a terrace floor, but again, a great deal will depend on how well the subfloor surface and grading are done to ensure drainage and a firm level bed for the floor. Setting in sand has several advantages, depending on each of the materials that are used. One of the most obvious is that, with just a little effort, the terrace can be changed or moved altogether. It may be increased in size and extended in several directions without the alteration being the least bit noticeable. All masonry terraces set in sand should be edged with treated wood or heavy aluminum dividing strips to separate the lawn and flower beds. These edging strips will allow you to run the lawn mower over the top of the strip and maintain the neat, crisp intersection of terrace and lawn. Sun screens, trellises, and arbors can be added to the terrace, but these will require separate footings for each column support.

Masonry terraces set in sand are durable, attractive, and require very little maintenance. They are also very easy to build, although some care is required in leveling the wet sand and setting the individual masonry units to be sure that a uniform slope and level surface are retained over the entire area with no projecting edges sticking up.

To keep weeds from growing up between the joints, strips of plastic, laid so that their edges overlap a few inches for drainage, should be placed under the sand bed. This will not prevent all weeds — for instance, those whose seeds are carried by the breeze, animals, or birds — but it will prevent any weeds that do appear from getting a strong root system going into the soil.

Brick

Brick set in sand is usually the first material that comes to mind when one thinks of a masonry unit, and brick is a fine choice because it is versatile, easy to work with, and handsome. The burnt red and brown colors set in sand are very easy on the eyes, even in bright sun, and bricks neither absorb heat nor reflect it, as concrete does. Their small size makes them easy to handle and pick up with one hand. Some of the heavier masonry materials, by contrast, require a lot of strenuous maneuvering. The small size of the brick is also excel-lent scale for a terrace of even very limited dimensions. If at a later time you decide that you want a more permanent terrace or a porch, the bricks can always be taken up and reused for floors or walls.

Five basic types of bricks are available at every brickyard: face brick, paving brick, firebrick, common brick, and used brick.

Face brick is a smooth-surfaced, very hard, square brick that is usually used on the outside wall of a structure. It is the most expensive, and since it is manufactured to be uniform, even, and square, it also tends to be very dull — unless you can find a load that has been rejected and returned, by a builder who did not like it because the color or texture varied (the very qualities that make it attractive for a terrace). This rejected brick will also be cheaper.

Paving brick varies from one manufacturer and brickyard to another. Although a form of face brick, it is usually more attractive for a terrace because it is more varied. Sometimes it is called "seconds," that is, it was made as face brick, but rejected because not of uniform color or size.

Firebrick, while always available and sometimes cheaper than face brick because of oversupply, should never be used for terraces or on an exterior. It is made only to resist heat on the floors and walls of fireplaces, and if used outdoors, will soon disintegrate. Many times firebrick is found mixed in with used brick. It should be returned to the brickyard and exchanged for bricks that will weather.

Common brick is just what the term implies. These bricks are used for any and all exterior brick construction. When face brick is put on an exterior, common brick is used as backup bricks. It is just as strong and durable as face brick, but doesn't have its even color and texture.

Common brick can be classified as wire-cut or sand-mold brick, depending on the method of manufacture. Wire-cut bricks tend to have a squarer outline but a rougher texture, many times with small pit marks on the surface. They age well, but are more difficult to clean than sand-mold bricks.

Sand-mold bricks are smooth and easily

cleaned, with softer edges than wire-cut bricks. Since they are made in a mold, one side is slightly larger than the other so they can slip easily out of the mold.

Both types of the common bricks are fired in an oven to make them hard, weatherproof, and durable. Because this firing process is an art as well as a science, the most attractive bricks are those that did not turn out "perfect."

Clinker bricks are common bricks that have been burned, either because they were too far in the back of the kiln or too far forward. And, just as with chocolate-chip cookies, these are usually the best ones. They will have dark, uneven, black patches and other irregularities; no two are quite alike. Though they are not straight or perfect in color, they are by far the most attractive new bricks you can use for a terrace or porch floor. However, because of their growing popularity, they may cost a bit more than the perfectly formed, perfectly fired common bricks.

Used brick, which at one time was readily available and cheap, is now more difficult to find and more expensive to buy than new common brick. It can cost from one to two cents more per brick because of the labor involved in cleaning and removing old mortar — unless you want to take on this chore yourself. Try cleaning a few bricks before you decide because it is dull, time-consuming labor that you may not find worth the savings.

Although the advantages of brick seem almost overwhelming, there are some disadvantages that should be noted. Brick set in sand will resettle a bit each winter, requiring some adjustments in the spring to correct uneven settling. Bricks are porous and absorb grease and oil. Paint or drops of paint spattered on them are almost impossible to clean, as are

An entrance path and terrace made of bricks set in a basket weave pattern.   Architect, A. J. Harmon, A.I.A.

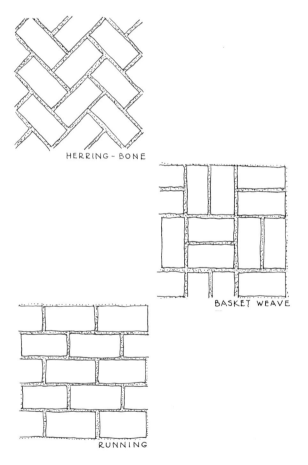

HERRING-BONE

BASKET WEAVE

RUNNING

Standard patterns of brick paving.

stains from grass, mildew, and spilled food. Some bricks crack and chip from freezing and thawing, and leave small holes that can collect dirt. These disadvantages must be weighed against the ease of installation and the overall appearance during the years of use a brick terrace will give you.

Slate

Slate set in sand is really only a variation of brick, except that slate offers a larger smooth surface between joints that can usually take the concentrated loads from tables and chair legs better than bricks, which are apt to crack or chip if the load is not centered.

However, because of its size and weight, slate is more difficult to lay than brick and the individual pieces harder to level, but it is also less liable to individual failure. Slate is more uneven than brick, and for this reason the joints will vary and in some places be much wider than in others. Because of this, you may want to leave large joints and fill them in with carefully cut strips of sod. The contrast between the slate and the sod, the hard stone against the soft green grass, can be very pleasant, and the terrace will drain and dry quickly after a rain.

The combination of slate and gravel is another interesting contrast, especially if the slate terrace is created as an island with gravel on all four sides and between the pieces of slate. The gravel will have to be swept back between the slate joints every once in a while, especially if there are active children around, but it makes an excellent interim terrace very inexpensively and with maximum dramatic effect. Gravel and sand can be reused later in foundations for a porch, and the slate can be used for the final porch floor.

A handsome terrace made of gravel surrounding a slate island.   Architects, Lewis and Harmon, A.I.A.

Slate terrace has white marble chips in the joints.

Architects, Lewis and Harmon, A.I.A.

The chief advantages of slate are its size, relatively light weight, and above all, its aesthetic value when no other material seems quite right for the house. It is not as porous as brick and can be cleaned much more easily than either brick or stone. Slate is available in shades of brown, red, and green, but by far the most attractive are the dark grays and black. These have an elegance that cannot be duplicated by any other material, and they provide a setting for the simplest planting that is seldom surpassed. Because of its dark color, slate is very restful in exposed areas where the terrace gets full sun.

Tile

Tile can be set in sand and used for a terrace, but it is usually not as successful as brick or slate. We normally associate tile, with its hard edges and precision surface, with a more substantial base than sand — if only because it is so expensive compared to the inexpensive sand on which it is placed. Any unevenness in the surface will be immediately detectable with tile, and with a sand base unevenness is almost inevitable. If you can afford tile, then you can afford to have a proper concrete base to install it on.

Flagstone

Unlike tile, flagstone is already uneven, and whether cut with squared edges or in irregular shapes, it lends itself to being set in sand. Its own weight will help keep it in place and the sand under it will fill in the shallow depths, creating a heavy, stable terrace. A 2-inch thickness should be the minimum when flagstones are to be set in sand. A lesser thickness may be used if the stones are to be set in concrete.

Because of the variable spaces in the joints of flagstone, sod or soil should be placed between the paving so that it is lower and not flush with the surface of the terrace, allowing water, surface dirt, and soil to drain off in the joints. The size of the flagstones can present a formidable appearance, which will be softened with sod — or better still, with very small rock garden plants, such as sedum or creeping thyme, planted in the joints. Plants will keep mud from streaking the terrace during heavy rains and will add welcome color and a gentleness so often lacking in flagstone terraces set in concrete. The kind and colors will be different, depending on the area in which you live and what is available locally.

Flagstone is probably the most expensive terrace material you will be dealing with, but it will last just about forever. Since it is so much more attractive set in sand with tiny flowers growing in the joints than it is set in hard concrete, the savings in concrete may help to balance the cost of the flagstone.

Paving Blocks

Cement paving blocks are available, and can be set in sand. Combined with gravel, or with poured concrete, and with sod blooming with small flowers between the joints, cement blocks can be very attractive, though you must consider first if the effort to make them so is worth it. The cost will be higher than for a floor of simple common brick, and though certain interesting effects can be obtained with cement blocks, you are still going to end up with a terrace set in sand having all the disadvantages of that slightly unstable material and none of the advantages of a permanent concrete terrace.

The precast cement paving blocks are larger than bricks, so fewer are needed and the work will go more quickly. However, they are much heavier than bricks, lack the small scale and interest of brick, and the only colors in which they are available are uninteresting washed-out pastel shades that will give a terrace a packaged plastic appearance.

You could cast your own cement paving in small blocks, and then set the blocks, one by one, in sand to create a terrace, but you would be ahead in time and money if you mixed cement, sand, and forms with water and gravel and poured your own concrete terrace.

There are other materials that can be set in sand to create a terrace besides the ones we have described here — adobe, wood rounds or cross-cut sections of tree trunks, railroad ties cut into wood blocks, and heavy locust or redwood planks left over from a construction site, for example — but these are regional products and availability and suitability vary from one area and town to the next.

Poured Floors

Terrace floors set in sand, however easy to do, however inexpensive and attractive, never give quite the permanence you need for a lasting addition to your home. Between the sand-based floor and the permanent, durable concrete terrace, there is another material that can be used, and this is asphalt.

Asphalt Paving: Long used for driveways, asphalt paving will, under certain circumstances, provide an acceptable, even an excellent, terrace. This type of terrace is not a do-it-yourself job, and that is one of the drawbacks of asphalt. You should have a paving contractor pour the terrace, using hot-mix asphalt over a graded area on a base of crushed stone. Asphalt is not a structural material and will crumble at the edges if not supported and edged with header boards. The asphalt should be tamped down tight at the edges to provide a crisp hard line between the terrace and the lawn and planting.

To keep weeds from growing through the asphalt (which they easily do), the ground under the terrace area should be treated with weed-killer or rock salt. Care should be taken to ensure that plantings next to the terrace do not have roots that reach into the treated soil.

Asphalt may be poured, rolled, and walked on in a few hours. Furniture and heavy traffic should be kept off it for a week to ten days, however, depending on weather conditions. Dining tables and chairs with sharp legs should not be used on an asphalt terrace; even fairly large furniture legs will leave an impression in the asphalt on hot summer days. If you plan to use a wrought-iron table and chairs, it may be better to pave the dining area in brick and bring the asphalt up to it. If asphalt is damaged, however, it is fairly easy to repair with ready-mixed asphalt that can be purchased in 50- and 100-pound bags.

There are asphalt mixes that can be bought, but these are so varied and sometimes so complicated that only after he has used them on paths and small areas should the average homeowner think of attempting to construct an asphalt terrace of any size. And even then, the results will be only moderately successful without the large heavy equipment used by the commercial contractor, who is used to doing driveways. Do not forget, incidentally, that the contractor will have to get this heavy equipment to the terrace area, which is usually not just off the drive, so be sure that there will be adequate space for his trucks and rollers, and be prepared for deep tire ruts in your lawn.

Asphalt will need to be repaired from time to time, and it will get very hot in the summer because it absorbs the sun's heat. It can be cooled quickly, however, by hosing it down with water, and in early spring and late fall the warmth it absorbs during the day can be very pleasant at night. Since much less asphalt is needed (only about 2 inches over a good crushed stone base) than concrete to cover the same area, asphalt is less expensive. But it will be only as good as the contractor who lays it, so before you hire anyone, get bids in writing and check on references. Also withhold 10 percent of the payment for at least one month to make sure that the contract is complied with in every detail.

Concrete Terraces: By far the best and most durable terraces you can build or have built for you are concrete. In addition, concrete can be reinforced and adequate footings easily poured, so that at a later date you can utilize all or part of the area of the terrace for an enclosed and roofed porch without going to extra expense for a new floor.

You can lay a concrete terrace yourself, or within a matter of hours you can have a large

A proper foundation (here using concrete and concrete block) must be provided for all terraces.

terrace poured. Again, the drainage and a good base of crushed rock must be established first, which, unless unusual site conditions exist, should be done by a contractor who will guarantee the work for very little additional money. Header boards should also be installed by the contractor, and if you are concerned about small cracks due to contraction and expansion, you can either have temperature reinforcing installed in the concrete or use an expansion joint every 8 feet.

If you want to lay the concrete yourself, it is an easy and simple matter — but only if you do it in small sections using a power mixer, which will do about 8 square feet of concrete, 3 inches thick, depending on the size of the mixer. The best way to lay concrete is to divide the terrace area into sections separated by redwood grids, each section being of a size that the mixer can fill in one batch. This way you can do as much or as little as you want at a time.

You can order concrete delivered by a truck that mixes it in transit, but if you are not experienced in working with concrete, having a small mountain of it delivered at once can turn into a frantic nightmare of attempting to spread it evenly and get the whole job finished before the concrete becomes too hard to work with. Another consideration is that the truck weighs an enormous amount and can crack your driveway. Also, if the terrace area is not very accessible from the street or highway, the cement truck will not be able to deliver the cement near enough to the work site without ruining the lawn, garden, and removing the limbs from a number of trees. Thus readymixed cement is not feasible in many cases. However, if a contractor is pouring the concrete, he will be able to tell if a truck is capable of getting in close enough without doing a lot of damage and how much concrete is needed.

The surface of the concrete can be finished in a number of textures from a hard glossy finish to a very rough one with exposed aggregate. The one you choose will depend on the design of your terrace and the use you intend to put it to.

Hard finish cleans very easily and can be made to look like marble, but it is really not very appropriate outdoors and can become so slippery and shiny that it will be a hazard for

Walled courtyard terrace with a simple concrete floor painted in rectangles.

Architects, Lewis and Harmon, A.I.A.

running youngsters and the elderly, who are not always so sure of their footing. However, if you think you may turn the terrace into an enclosed porch one day, you might want to use hard finish because it is so easy to clean. There are slip-resistant paints that will cut the hazard somewhat, but still, this finish should be avoided if possible.

For a hard finish, the surface of the concrete should be smoothed with a steel trowel after it has been allowed to set for a half-hour. Then it should be troweled a second time, and even a third and fourth for a really hard surface.

A smooth finish, less hard and not so glossy, can be obtained. This is called a wood-float finish. The concrete is simply gone over and

Elegant terrace floor uses river-washed stones set in cement.

with water, washing away the top layer of sand and cement to expose the small stones used as aggregate. This sort of finish can be attractive (depending on how attractive the aggregate is), and it is about as rough as you can get concrete to be, but it is difficult to clean, furniture wobbles on it, and after a time it tends to lose its rustic charm. Before tackling a whole terrace, you should practice exposing the aggregate on a small piece of experimental concrete.

There are colorings for concrete, but none is really attractive or successful and most are expensive. Painting concrete is the best way to color it, although new exterior concrete paint is expensive. Paint goes on very easily and quickly, dries in an hour, and even enamels can be cleaned up with soap and water. Concrete must cure for at least six months before it is painted, no matter what type of paint is used, or the paint will not adhere. So if you want to have your terrace painted and planted and in tiptop shape for spring, you should have it poured by October.

Porch Floors

A conventional porch floor would not normally be set on sand, although for additional drainage and heightened moisture content in the air, it could be. Examples would be a porch that is also used as an orangery or a greenhouse that is also a breakfast room. Usually a porch will have a poured concrete floor, which can be finished and painted as concrete, or laid over with brick, slate, or tile.

Laying brick, flagstone, slate, or tile on a concrete base does take some skill. Probably the most difficult material is flagstone, the easiest, tile with brick and slate somewhere in between. It is usually a mistake to spend a fortune in money and time putting down the perfect flagstone or brick finish on a porch floor because after the first season of admiring what can be seen of it between lounge chairs and the coffee tables, some member of the family will decide that it is too cold and hard looking and it will be covered with a rush, straw, or another form of outdoor carpet.

Tile

Ceramic tile may be the possible exception

smoothed a second time with a wooden trowel.

For a really rough texture, where there is danger of people slipping, you can use a broom finish. Different textures can be obtained, depending on the type of broom used to rough the concrete. If you have decided that you want to mix and pour the concrete yourself, some very interesting effects can be obtained by dividing the terrace into a grid pattern and changing the direction of the brush stroke used to texture the concrete in different areas of the grid. Textured concrete will collect dust and be more difficult to clean, but on some grades and steps it is essential for safety, although small children who fall on it can receive a scraping.

A very interesting finish for concrete can be had by exposing the aggregate. The aggregate is the rough stone mixed with the cement and sand that helps bond the concrete and allows masons to use less of the more expensive cement. Before the concrete has hardened, when it is still "green," the surface is removed by scrubbing it with a wire brush and flushing it

Porch floor of painted concrete.

Architect, A. J. Harmon, A.I.A.

because it can be so highly decorative in itself, and it does not have the cool harshness of masonry. Since tile is thin and manufactured to precise measurements, it is easier to level. It is a simple matter to grout between tiles, and any extra grout or spills can quickly and easily be cleaned up.

Quarry tile has no glaze and is sold in many different shapes and sizes — which is its main attraction — and the subtle color differences that are due to various temperatures when the tile was fired can be quite interesting. Some ceramic floor tiles (derived from Spanish, Italian, English, Mexican, or Dutch tile) can be used on protected porches, and in warmer climates. Although expensive, they add distinction and scale to the smallest porch. But some are very slippery when wet and others do not weather well in freezing climates, so make certain before you buy that the tile you want will perform as you expect it to in your area.

Slate

If you use only the grays and blacks, or slate of different shades of the same color, you will have a very handsome and sturdy floor. The scale and interest can vary according to size, and you can alter the standard masonry appearance by using wider joints and filling them with pebbles that complement the color of the slate.

Finishing

Indoor-outdoor carpet may be used if you feel you must have a soft surface for children to play on, and it will help to quiet a noisy porch.

Paint on concrete is the easiest, and in many ways the best, way to finish the floor of a porch. It is slip-resistant, will dry in an hour, and the new water-soluble enamels wear quite well. Whether you painted simple squares or a complicated design, touching up the worn places each spring takes only about an hour and the brushes can be cleaned with water and soap.

Every porch floor should be sloped to the exterior wall so that rainwater coming through the screens will be drained off through weep holes. A slope of ⅛ inch to the foot is adequate for all but the most unusual conditions. Place screened weep holes every 4 feet on the lower edge of the floor.

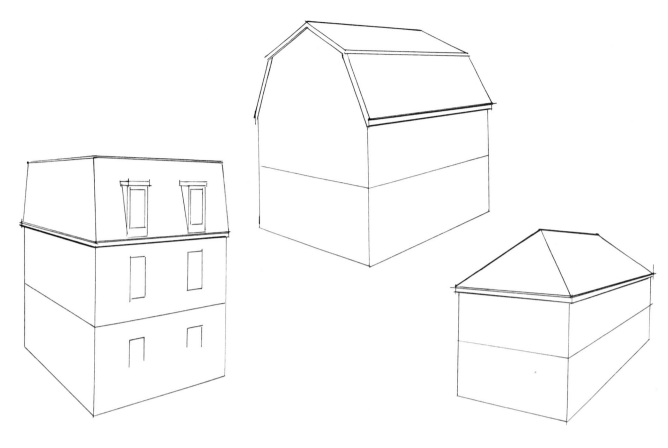

A Mansard, gambrel, and hip roof.

Porch Roofs

When designing the roof of a porch, the roof supports and columns must be taken into consideration; without them there could be no roof. Space the columns close enough so screening material can be stretched between them with no waste, or provide an intermediate and nonstructural support for the screen. Also use a spacing that sliding glass or French doors will conveniently fit into so that if one day you decide to glass in the porch, you will not have to change existing supports and columns or have custom-made doors and windows fitted.

The type and kind of finish you use on the porch roof will probably be the same as that on the house itself, although you may want to take this opportunity to change the roofing material on your house. The kind of material you use for roofing will depend to some extent on the kind of roof you are using and the slope. You may also want to do more with the roof than simply use it to cover the porch; for instance, you could add a second-floor porch or sun deck on top of the porch, or the roof of the porch could be used to extend the bedroom area or add valuable storage to the second floor.

Types of Roofs

There are many roof styles, but the six you are likely to be dealing with in adding a porch are: gable, shed, hip, and flat roofs (the most common, in that order, in most parts of the country); gambrel, which is Dutch, German, Swedish, or Flemish, depending on the angles of the slopes; and Mansard. We will take up this last roof first because imitations of it are so common.

Mansard was a French architect who developed this system of roofing in Paris in the seventeenth century to get around the zoning laws in effect at that time. This type of roof looks rather silly on anything but a French townhouse, and porches are impossible to add

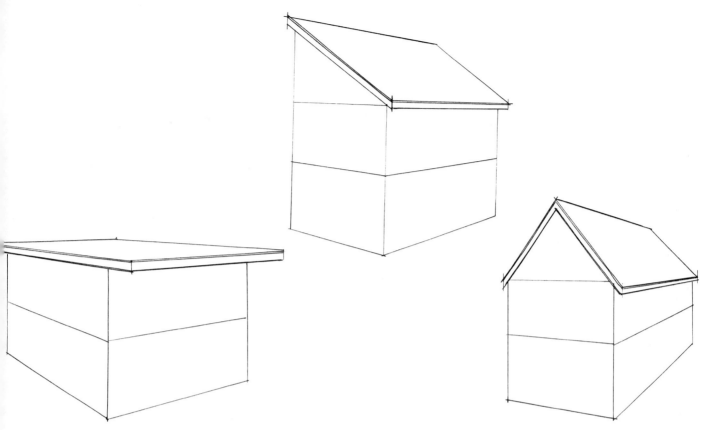

A flat, shed, and gable roof.

without looking equally ridiculous — unless you admit that fact and add a porch with a flat roof.

Gambrel roofs have two slopes on each side. This type of roof has no European precedents; it was developed in this country as a way to gain space on an upper floor with the use of little material. Porches are difficult to add to a house with this kind of roof, except on the side. Usually the lower of the two pitches is used, or the porch addition is flat-roofed. Porches can be added to the front or back using a gable or a shed-roof addition, but great care must be taken to preserve the original lines of the house.

Hip roofs are Mediterranean in origin. The style was developed so that a low slope could be maintained on all sides of the roof so the clay tiles that were used at that time for roofing material would hold. Additions to hip-roofed houses should have hip roofs if the character of the house is to be maintained.

Flat roofs should, in general, be used on addi-tions to houses with flat roofs, although for ad-ded interest and character, it is usually best to make the height of the addition above or below that of the existing house.

Shed roofs are the least expensive roofs to construct on any addition. The name is derived from the inexpensive farm buildings that used this type of roof, and they are as American as apple pie. When correctly used, a shed roof is both handsome and functional, as witnessed by the salt-box Early American homes and the purely contemporary construction of today. A widespread misuse is on a porch against the side of a gable house that has a low pitch.

Gable roofs are the most common on both one- and two-story houses. Porches added to the front or side of the house should maintain the same slope.

Roofing Materials

Asphalt shingles are at present the most widely used material for roofs with a pitch of a minimum of 3 inches to the foot. Do not use asphalt on roof pitches lower than that, and always use the self-sealing tab asphalt shingle so it will not blow or flutter in the wind. The 235-pound shingle is the lightest that should be used — the number of shingles required to cover a "square," or 100 square feet, and weighing 235 pounds. Asphalt shingles are not fireproof; heavier grades are better for color retention and weathering.

Built-up asphalt or hot-pitch roofs are used on low-pitched or flat roofs. Hot asphalt is alternated with layers of felt and topped with gravel. If a second-floor porch or terrace is desired, the roof can be covered with duckboards to keep foot traffic and furniture from puncturing the built-up roof. Or, tile or slate may be applied over the roof if the structure is reinforced to carry the additional load.

Wood shingles are more expensive than asphalt, but they last twenty years or more and provide a handsome roof for either traditional or modern styles of architecture. They also burn readily and some codes prohibit them.

Wood shakes are thicker wood shingles. They cost more and last longer, but they have the same advantages and disadvantages as wood shingles. Hank-split shakes are much more rugged, with a great deal more texture.

Asbestos shingles are fireproof and must be used on a minimum pitch of 5 inches to the foot. Although they are heavy and weigh 250 to 600 pounds per square, they are brittle and should not be walked on or used where they might be damaged.

Aluminum shingle roofing is fireproof, but it is expensive and used mostly for commercial work.

Corrugated metal of either aluminum or steel can be used in conjunction with translucent fiberglass panels to light dark corners of a porch or areas over windows. The steel must be painted and each sheet requires a pitch of 3 inches to the foot.

10
Stairs

Changes in level, on either a porch or a terrace, are almost inevitable, not only so the surface of the floor can drain properly to prevent water from backing up inside the house, but also so the outdoor living spaces will be more accessible on difficult sites. But stairs have another purpose besides function, and that is to inspire our imaginations and challenge our minds. This change in atmosphere, in orientation, in seeing things from a different level is so universal that it has become a motif in literature, music, art, religion, and business regardless of the age or culture. The Egyptians built pyramids, the Aztecs built many-storied temples, gods lived on high mountains or in the sky. Children climb ladders simply because they are there, businessmen climb the ladder of success, judges hand down sentences, there is a stairway to paradise, one to Heaven, and no lady in distress ever appealed from the first floor — she was either up in a tower or down in a dungeon, and the duel to save her always involved a staircase. Every opera or drama with a happy ending has the hero and/or heroine either floating down or rushing up a staircase to light, life, and joy. It is not at all strange that steps are called a flight of stairs. Who can resist the beckoning stairway at the Paris Opéra, the gangplank of a ocean liner, the winding stair of a lighthouse, or even sitting on top of the kitchen ladder to have lunch when there is a comfortable chair a few feet away?

Design

The design of stairs is often more exciting than where they lead, and what you find at the top may not be as important as the climb. Stairs can be seemingly effortless; this is part of design and should be considered along with the durability and safety of the construction before the work is begun. In any run of stairs, all risers and treads should be the same size because the slightest difference interrupts the rhythm of your step and can cause you to break your stride and trip. It is mentally tiring and physically dangerous if your mind has to consciously anticipate the next step. The height of the rise and the depth of the run also determine the ease with which a stair can be climbed or descended. The height of a riser on an exterior stair should not exceed 6 inches. The tread, or run, is variable, but should never be smaller than 11 inches.

Exterior stairs should never be permitted to end like this.

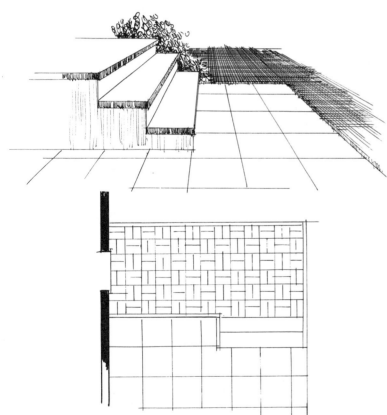

The extra cost of concrete to front the stairs and provide a walkway is almost nothing.
With some additional expense the entrance could be made very attractive as shown in the plan.

Architects use a quick rule of thumb to check the design of interior stairs; the run plus twice the rise should be equal to 25, or the run multiplied by the rise should be equal to 75. On exterior stairs, however, this rule of thumb has great latitude because there are no restrictions on head room and few on the length of the run and width of the stair. The rhythm of a stair may not be suitable to everyone's taste, which varies from that of the teenager who likes to take two steps at a time to that of an elderly person who prefers a more leisurely pace.

Do not have steps ending in the middle of nowhere, or as an afterthought (as illustrated in the photograph on the left), when with only a few seconds' more time and a few more pennies a ludicrous situation can be avoided. The association of entrance terrace and steps to a front door can be avoided simply by extending the terrace to meet the bottom of the steps. For several dollars more, the stairs could have been made into a stylish and important enhancement of the front door.

Kind of Steps

Exterior steps to any door should be an absolute minimum of 4 feet wide, and in most cases, 5 feet wide. This will allow two people to help a third person up or down the stairs. A width of 5 feet will permit two people to assist a third in a wheelchair up or down the steps. A 5-foot-wide stair is hardly lavish when you consider that most front doors are 3 feet wide, meaning there will be only an extra foot on each side for the steps.

There should always be more than one step except at thresholds where a change in levels is expected. Even one 6-inch-high step is safer if broken into two 3-inch-high steps, because one step can so easily be overlooked.

Stairs can add or detract from the charm of the best-designed porch or terrace, whether it is small and built of inexpensive materials or large and built without regard to a budget. If the difference in level from the house to the porch or terrace is considerable, broad wide steps may be used as a major piece of furniture. Wide steps offer an opportunity to change cushions, potted plants, and accessories to different locations. If the space is limited, a combination of one or two sets of stairs can transform a simple and dull access into an entrance. Space under the landing can be used for storing garden furniture in off seasons and any number of porch accessories.

Corner steps may be useful and decorative in many instances; however, they take up valuable space, are subject to uneven settling, and are very difficult to provide with secure handrails. A handrail is not required for all stairs, but it, or some kind of support, is necessary for toddlers and the elderly on all stairs with more than two risers.

Curved stairs suffer from the same disadvantages as corner stairs, although they do not take up porch or terrace space and hand support can be obtained along the sides when necessary. Curved stairs are more expensive than straight steps in any material, and the design element introduced — the curve — should be repeated elsewhere in the terrace and garden or it will look odd and isolated.

Construction

Porch and terrace steps should have the same sturdy foundations that the structure they lead up to has. The loads on the stairs will be more concentrated, however, and since stairs are usually on a slope, even greater care should be exercised in their design. Every material dictates its own particular amount and depth of foundation. Second only to durability is lighting, which must be considered along with the design and construction of each staircase.

Building Materials

Wood steps are usually first to come to mind for a porch or terrace because wood is perhaps the most available material and the easiest to work with. Wood steps are suitable for interior work, for covered and screened porches, and for wood decks, but they should be used sparingly in other situations. Usually a gravel terrace, if

Inexpensive wooden stairs can also be attractive if well designed.   Architect, A. J. Harmon, A.I.A.

Frank Russell

it requires steps, would have wood steps because of the general instability of gravel. The combination can look very good because of the header boards that must be used to contain the gravel.

Wood steps should be built with the bottom resting on a concrete foundation. Treads should be sloped to drain, with spaces of ¼ to ½ inch between planks on horizontal surfaces. Most wood will not weather the outdoors unless it is preserved with stain or paint. Of the two, stain is better because it will last longer and is not slippery when wet, as so many paints are.

Gravel steps to a gravel terrace are a possibility, but usually wood steps would be better because gravel tends to be too unstable.

Sod steps are very economical and quick to build. They should be wide enough so that you can change the path that is used through them each week or they will show wear.

Brick steps require a base of either poured concrete or concrete block, but are fairly easy to build and are the only kind of steps that should be used with a brick terrace or porch.

Slate steps can be very effective when used with a slate terrace or porch, or when combined with a gravel terrace that has a slate island in it. Brick and slate are, of course, an age-old combination, as in brick risers and slate treads.

Tile steps can be quite handsome, but are expensive and tend to be very slippery when wet. The tile should be applied over poured concrete. To reduce the cost and improve the safety of the steps, tile may be used only on the riser and concrete on the tread. The concrete can be painted with a nonslip paint.

Flagstone steps are very difficult to do and are very expensive. They must be laid over a concrete base, and unless the treads are very wide and the stones very smooth and carefully trimmed, they will form an uneven surface that is difficult to climb.

Asphalt steps are inexpensive and, with wooden risers, are very simple to build. They should have a base of crushed stone and be well compacted to minimize wear. Asphalt steps are excellent for long runs with 2-by-4s used as risers for terrace or garden steps.

Concrete steps, being the basis for all masonry, are the most common of all masonry steps; certainly they are the most foolproof and durable. Because of their weight, they should have a footing and be poured on a base of crushed stone. Treads should be slightly sloped to drain water, and a rough texture will prevent them from being too slippery when painted.

Glossary

Alligatoring: An advanced form of cracking and checking on the surface of paint where it has pulled away from the wood.

Anchor Bolt: A heavy bolt imbedded in masonry to secure a wooden sill to a foundation.

Angle Iron: A strip of metal in the form of an "L," used to support masonry over openings.

Apron: A finished piece of wood below the sill of a window that covers the rough edge of plaster.

Arbor: An open-roofed and open-sided passage for the support of vines, fruit, or flowers.

Arcade: A covered passage open on one side and supported by arches on a series of columns.

Asbestos Shingles: Fireproof shingles of asbestos used for siding and roofs.

Ash Dump: A metal frame or drawer placed in the floor of a fireplace through which ashes can be disposed of.

Asphalt: A mineral pitch or tar used on built-up roofs and, the exteriors of foundation walls to waterproof them. It is also used as a base that, when combined with other materials, can be laid on driveways and terraces.

Asphalt Shingles: Shingles combining asphalt pitch and coated with mineral granules used for siding and roofing.

Atrium: A large, completely enclosed terrace or garden open to the sky, with the principal rooms of the house arranged around it.

Back Filling: Soil and broken stones used to level around the foundation walls and provide a slope for water to be drained away from the house walls.

Balcony: A small cantilevered projection with access from a door on an upper floor of a house.

Baluster: One of the short posts used to make up a balustrade, and part of a railing of a stair or balcony.

Balustrade: A railing made up of posts connected at the top by a handrail.

Base Shoe: A strip of molding nailed to the baseboard next to the floor.

Batts: Insulating material composed of mineral fiber with a vapor barrier on one side, sized to fit between stud walls and joists.

Beam: A large piece of timber or metal used to support the floor joists.

Bearing Plate: A metal plate placed under a column or beam to distribute the weight of the load on the structural member.

Bearing Wall: A wall that carries the load from floor joists and partitions above it.

Belvedere: A garden structure built on a high point of land overlooking a view.

Blistering: A failure in the surface of paint in which the paint film pulls away from the surface painted.

Board Foot: A unit of measure for lumber. One board foot would be a piece of lumber 1 foot square and approximately 1 inch thick.

Bond: The pattern in which brickwork is done.

Bower: A playful garden structure, usually of semipermanent construction.

Box Out: A term meaning to cover columns or beams with another material to improve their appearance.

Break Ground: The first work done when an addition or new building is started.

Breezeway: A covered passage between two buildings, usually between a house and garage, open on both sides.

Brick Veneer: A layer of brick one brick thick attached to the surface of a wall, but carrying no load except its own weight.

Bridging: Pieces of wood or metal straps crisscrossed between joists to stiffen them and hold them in place.

Building Line: The limit to which you are permitted to build or extend your house in relation to the edge of your property.

Built-up Beam: A beam formed by nailing or bolting two or more planks together to increase their strength.

Built-up Column: A column made of more than one piece of lumber.

Built-up Roof: A roofing material used on flat roofs consisting of a number of plys of roofing felt and hot pitch topped with gravel.

BX Cable: Electric cable encased in flexible metal or heavy plastic.

Cabana: A poolside garden house used for changing and showering.

Cantilever: The structural overhang projecting beyond the supporting wall or column.

Cased Opening: A finished opening with trim, but not having a door.

Casement: A window hinged on its vertical edge.

Casing: Framework around a window or door.

Casino: Small garden structure built for conversation and games.

Cement: A mixture of portland cement, sand, and water used as mortar.

Chalking: The powdering of the top surface of paint.

Check: Hairline crack in paint or wood.

Cinder Block: A building block made of cement and cinders and light in weight.

Clapboard: Long boards, thin on top and thicker on the bottom edge, used horizontally for siding.

Clerestory: A wall containing a window raised above surrounding roofs.

Cloister: A covered passage open on one side and surrounding a court.

Colonnade: A decorative and roofed passage open on both sides.

Concrete: A mixture of cement, sand, water, and gravel.

Condensation: Warm, moist air changing to drops of water on a cold surface such as glass or metal.

Coping: The top course of a masonry wall.

Corner Boards: Vertical boards used to trim the corner of an exterior frame wall.

Cornice: The decorative construction at the intersection of the roof and side wall at the eaves.

Corrosion: The rusting or oxidation of two metals by contact and interaction with oxygen.

Court: An open terrace surrounded by house walls on all four sides.

Courtyard: An open terrace surrounded on three sides by house walls and protected on the fourth side by a wall.

Crawling: A defect in the paint film in which it breaks, separates into globules.

Crawl Space: The unexcavated space enclosed by the foundation walls under the first floor of a house.

Creosote: A coal-tar product which causes treated wood to be impervious to insects and weathering.

Dead Load: The weight of structure and finishing materials carried by joist and structural walls.

Deck: A raised wooden terrace.

Delamination: Separation of plywood plys due to moisture.

Design: Drawings showing the plan, elevation, and sections used in the construction of any work done on a structure.

Detail Drawing: A separate drawing showing special features of construction.

Dormer Window: A vertical window in a sloping roof.

Double-hung Window: A window with an upper and lower vertical sliding sash.

Down Light: An incandescent light fixture, recessed into the ceiling so that only the floor under the fixture is illuminated.

Dress: To smooth and finish wood or masonry.

Dressed-size Lumber: A term referring to the actual size of lumber. For instance, a 2-by-4 stud is actually 1⅝ inches by 3⅝ inches.

Dry Stone Wall: A masonry wall laid without mortar.

Dry Wall: This term generally refers to interior wall finish without plaster. However, it usually means ⅜- or ½-inch gypsum wallboard or Sheetrock with the joints taped and spackled.

Dutch Door: A door divided horizontally so the top half may be opened while the lower section remains closed.

Easement: An acquired right to use part of land belonging to someone else.

Eaves: The part of the roof that projects over the side walls.

Efflorescence: White powder which forms on the surface of brick or masonry.

Elevation: A geometrical drawing of the side of a house or house wall.

Escutcheon: A metal plate or shield placed around and behind the doorknob and keyhole to protect the wood of the door.

Facade: The exterior appearance of a house or elevation.

Fascia: The flat horizontal board at the outer face of the cornice.

Fenestration: The arrangement and design of doors and windows in a wall.

Finish Floor: Brick, tile, slate, or other material laid over the base or subfloor.

Fixed Glass: A stationary window.

Flashing: Sheet metal used at all intersections of walls, roofs, changes in materials, and over doors and windows, to prevent water from leaking into the house.

Flat Roof: A horizontal roof with or without just enough slope to drain off water.

Floating: Bringing a smooth finish to cement or concrete.

Florida Room: A combination room, terrace, and greenhouse.

Footing: The foundation for a column or wall which distributes the weight carried over a greater area. Footings are usually concrete and are placed below the frost line to prevent structural damage from freezing.

Form Lumber: The boards used to build forms.

Forms: These are enclosures made with wood or metal to shape and hold the wet (green) concrete until it has set and dried sufficiently to support itself and imposed loads.

Frame Construction: The type of building made of lumber, using wood studs, joists, and beams.

Framing: The process of putting together the lumber to form the house.

French Door: One or a pair of doors with glazed panels extending the full length.

Front Elevation: A drawing of the front view of a house.

Furring: The act of applying furring strips to provide an air space between structural walls and the interior finish or to level the surface.

Furring Strips: Narrow strips of wood or metal.

Gable: The triangular portion of an end wall contained between the sloping eaves of a roof.

Gable Roof: A ridged roof ending at one or both ends in a gable.

Gallery: A roofed passage open on one or both sides for the display of sculpture.

Gambrel Roof: A ridge roof with a double slope, the lower slope being the steeper.

Gazebo: A summerhouse in a garden.

Glaze: The installation of glass in windows and doors.

Glazed Tile: Masonry tile with a hard glossy surface on one side.

Grade: The ground level around a building.

Grading: Filling in around a building with earth so water will drain away from the foundations. It can also mean the smoothing and proper leveling of property.

Green Concrete: Concrete that has achieved its initial set, but that is still wet.

Grout: A cement mixture used to fill joints of slate, tile, brick, and other masonry.

Hardpan: A compacted layer of earth and clay which is dense and difficult to excavate.

Hardware: Doorknobs, locks, hinges, and other metal used on doors and windows.

Header Boards: Those boards that are used and left set to separate gravel or other terrace material from surrounding earth.

Hydrostatic Head: Water pressure from a high water table pressing on the underside of slabs and foundations.

I-Beam: A steel beam in the shape of a capital "I" used to support walls and roofs where structural walls have been removed.

Insect Screen: Screen cloth used in windows and on porches to keep out insects.

Jalousie Window: Unframed strips of glass set in a series opening from the bottom to prevent rain from entering. Often used to glaze walls and doors in a Florida room.

Jamb: A vertical side post used in framing a door or window.

Joist: One of a number of timbers used to support floors and ceilings.

Kiln-dried: A term used to refer to lumber that

has been dried in a kiln with controlled heat and humidity to artificially season it.

Knee Wall: A low wall in the attic running parallel to the ridge closing off unusable space.

Lally Column: A round steel pipe, usually 4 inches in diameter and sometimes filled with concrete, used to support beams.

Laminate: Built-up layers of wood or other material held in place with glue or tar.

Lanai: Hawaiian term for porch.

Lath: Small strips of wood about ⅜ inch thick and 1 inch wide, used to support plaster, seal cracks, and build decorative screens.

Lath House: Small garden house with its walls made of decorative lath.

Leader: A pipe or downspout to carry off rain.

Lean-to: A small addition to a house or garage having a shed roof which is supported by the other structure.

Lien: A legal claim against the owner of a house by a contractor who has not been paid for work and materials supplied.

Light: A single windowpane.

Lineal Foot: A line 1 foot long, as distinguished from a square foot or a cubic foot.

Lintel: A steel, wood, or stone beam placed horizontally over an opening to support the wall above it.

Live Load: The weight of furniture and occupants on joist and structural walls.

Loft: A room or platform in a roof.

Loggia: An arcade covered by a roof and having one open and one closed side.

Lumber: Timber cut into standard sizes.

Mastic: A thick adhesive used for bedding glass, setting tile, and repairing roofs.

Metal Ties: Steel straps coated with portland cement and used to tie brick or stone veneer to frame walls.

Millwork: Woodwork that has been finished, machined, and partly assembled at the mill.

Modular Design and Construction: Using a module of 4 feet, residential work is more economical and there is less waste. Studs and joists are placed on 16-inch centers with a ceiling height of 8 feet, which per-mits plywood and interior finishes to be used without cutting and waste since they are manufactured in sheets 4 by 8 feet.

Module: A unit of measure used by architects and designers.

Nail Sizes: The size of a nail is indicated by the word "penny," which was originally the price per hundred. Sizes may vary slightly from standard because of different manufacturers, but in general a 4d (the d means penny) nail is 1½ inches long, the 6d is 2 inches, the 8d is 2½ inches, the 10d is 3 inches, the 20d is 4 inches, and the 60d is 6 inches.

Nailing Strips: Pieces of wood to which finish material is nailed. Similar to furring strips.

Nonbearing Walls: Partitions that do not carry the weight from overhead walls, partitions, or joists; they support only their own weight and divide space into rooms.

Nosing: The rounded edge of a stair tread.

Obscure Glass: Glass that does not permit a clear view through it.

Orangery: A high-ceilinged, glassed-in porch or greenhouse on the south side of a house used for growing oranges and other fruit indoors out of season. Many times these are also used as breakfast rooms.

Orientation: The location of the house regarding the direction in which it faces.

Outlet: Electrical term meaning the place where a fixture, plug, or switch is connected.

Overhang: The projection of a floor or roof over an outside wall.

Overloading: Placing too much weight on a beam, column, or floor.

Panel Box: The electrical fuse and switch box once used and still contained in some houses. In general, these have been replaced by circuit breakers and are no longer permitted.

Party Wall: A structural wall shared by two houses.

Patio: A terrace surrounded on all four sides by house walls.

Pavilion: An elegant open-walled structure built in the garden and not attached to the house.

Penny: The term used for nail sizes.

Pergola: A garden structure similar to an arbor.

Perspective Drawing: A sketch of a house made from a particular location so that if a photograph of the house were taken from the same place you would see the same thing.

Piazza: An Italian word for porch.

Pilaster: A column attached to a wall.

Pillar: A supporting masonry shaft made of smaller pieces of marble, stone, or brick; differs from a column in that a column is one piece of solid material, such as steel.

Pitch: Various combinations of coal tar, insoluble in water and used in plumbing and other construction work.

Plank: A heavy piece of timber thicker than a board, usually 1½ inches thick and more than 6 inches wide.

Plate: A 2-by-4 or larger piece of lumber placed on top of a stud wall or masonry so that joists and rafters may be attached to it.

Pointing: Finishing of joints in a masonry wall.

Porch: A roofed and floored outdoor living space attached to the house.

Porte Cochere: A covered automobile entrance connecting the driveway to the front door.

Portico: An open space attached to a house, as a porch, or completely detached, with a roof supported by columns.

Portland Cement: A mixture of silica, lime, and alumina mixed together and fired in a kiln. The clinkers are then ground fine to produce a strong hydraulic cement.

Post: An upright column.

Primary Colors: The three primary colors are red, yellow, and blue. The secondary colors are mixtures of two primary colors, and are orange, green, and purple.

Priming: The first coat of paint, usually called a special primer, on wood or metal to make a hard opaque surface that will take additional coats of paint well.

Quarry Tile: Machine-made unglazed tile, usually of a reddish-brown color.

Quarry-faced Masonry: A rough squared stone with the face as it was split in the quarry.

Quarter-round: A molding that is a quarter of a circle.

Rabbet: A section cut out of wood and timber to receive another board cut to fit.

Rafter: The sloping member of the roof structure that runs from the plate to the ridge.

Reinforced Concrete: Concrete that has been given greater strength by imbedding steel bars in it.

Rendering: A finished perspective painting of the house in ink, watercolor, or some other medium.

Retaining Wall: A wall built to hold back the soil.

Ridge: The top of a roof where two slopes meet and intersect.

Riser: The vertical board under the tread of a step; also the distance measured vertically between two treads.

Rough Floor: A subfloor that will serve as a base for the finished flooring material.

Rough Opening: An unfinished opening in which the window and door frames will be placed.

Rounds: Sections of paving material cut from tree trunks perpendicular to the grain.

Rustic: Imitation primitiveness.

Saddle: A board or marble covering the joint on the floor where one material changes to another.

Sash: The frame for one or more windowpanes.

Sawtooth Roof: A type of roof that admits light to the interior of a structure.

Scale: There are two kinds of scale. Architects do drawings to scale, relating to the full-size house: i.e., scale ¼ inch = 1 foot means that ¼ inch on the drawings represents 1 foot on the actual house. The architect does this measuring and drawing with an expensive ruler also called a scale. Architects also speak of scale in relation to appropriateness and proportion of elements in the design of a house. If something is out of scale, it is either too large or too small for the rest of the house.

Section: A drawing of the house seen from a given point as if it were a loaf of bread cut down the middle.

Shake: A heavy wood shingle.

Sheathing: Plywood or boards nailed to the studs and rafters on the exterior of the house as a foundation for the finish siding and roofing.

Shed Roof: A roof sloping in one direction with a single pitch.

Shim: A thin, tapered piece of shingle that is used in leveling work.

Shingle: Thin pieces of wood or other material that is tapered and used to cover walls and roofs.

Shore: A piece of timber used as a temporary support.

Sill: The lowest horizontal member of a frame supporting a house, or the lowest member under a door or window.

Sleeper: Strip of wood laid over rough concrete floors so a finished wood floor can be applied.

Sleeping Porch: An unheated open or closed porch on an upper floor of a house used for sleeping outdoors.

Soffit: The underside of overhangs.

Solarium: A room with glass walls and some glass in the ceiling.

Span: The distance between supports for a joist.

Stoop: A small roofed projection at the entrance to a house.

Stud: A vertical piece of lumber, usually a 2-by-4, used in concert with others to form walls and partitions.

Summerhouse: A detached garden structure with a roof and walls, generally rustic in character.

Sun Parlor: An enclosed and glazed sitting room on the south.

Sun Porch: An enclosed porch on the south.

Sun Room: A room facing south with 50 percent or more of its walls glazed.

Terrace: A paved open space used for outdoor living.

Terrazzo: A mixture of marble chips and cement, ground and polished smooth.

Three-way Switch: An electric switch that allows an electric fixture to be controlled from two separate places.

Tie Beam: A beam that prevents the spreading apart of rafters.

Toenailing: Nailing at an angle to attach one piece of lumber to another.

Top Plate: The horizontal member nailed to the top of a partition.

Transite: Manufactured fireproof sheets made of a combination of asbestos and cement.

Trellis: Screens made of lath to support vines and flowers.

Trowel: A flat steel tool used to spread and smooth cement and mortar.

Valley: The intersection of two roofs.

Vapor Barrier: Material used to keep moisture from penetrating walls.

Variance: Written permission from a zoning board to build or remodel in a manner that is acceptable in this one instance only.

Veneered Wall: Brick or stone that is not bonded together, but attached to a frame wall with clips, and does not carry any load but its own weight.

Veranda: A Hindu word meaning porch.

Wainscot: A lining or paneling for the lower part of an interior wall.

Weather Strip: A flange of metal or plastic covering joints to keep out drafts around doors and windows.

Wet Wall: A term used to refer to walls that have soil pipes, hot- and cold-water pipes, and vents in them.

Winders: Treads of stairs shaped like triangles and used at corners.

Index